smart investing
@ your library®

A partnership between American Library Association
and FINRA Investor Education Foundation

ALA American Library Association

FINra
Investor Education
FOUNDATION

FINRA is proud to support the American Library Association

FINANCIAL INTELLIGENCE

GETTING BACK TO BASICS AFTER AN ECONOMIC MELTDOWN

BY

JACOB GOLD, CFP®

WITH JEFF RATTINER

STERLING & ROSS PUBLISHERS

NEW YORK

Published by
Sterling & Ross Publishers
New York, NY 10001
www.sterlingandross.com

Cover design by Greg-Paul Malone and Caroline Maher.
Book design by Rachel Trusheim.

Library of Congress Cataloging-in-Publication Data

Gold, Jacob H.
  Financial intelligence : getting back to the basics after an economic meltdown / Jacob H. Gold.
    p. cm.
  ISBN 978-0-9821391-3-4 (pbk.)
  1. Finance, Personal--United States. 2. Retirement income--United States--Planning. 3. Retirement--Economic aspects--United States. 4. Retirement--United States--Planning. I. Title.

  HG179.G64 2009
  332.024'0140973--dc22

                                    2009017688

Printed in the United States of America.

I dedicate this book to my wife, Sara,
son, Kelvin, and daughter, Savanna.
Thank you for all your love and support.

ACKNOWLEDGMENTS

I wish to thank my father, Bill Gold, and grandfather, Everett Gold, who taught me everything I know about the investment world. A special thanks to my amazing family for allowing me the time and energy to get this project off the ground and finished. I would also like to thank my oldest brother, Kelly, who always was and always will be my hero. You made the world a better place and you will always be remembered. I love you and miss you desperately. Thank you to everyone else in my life that has supported me and has helped me in more ways than I can mention: Sharon Gold, John and Sandy Whaley, Jill Gold, Wyatt Gold, Mike and Brittany Gold, Lisa and Luke Gold, Mark Whaley, Jeff Whaley, Sherry Kowitz, Ida Chaidez, Marty Matyas, Neal Thompson, Mike Cochell, David Scheur, Barbara Gill, Creighton Barker, Adam Hiniker and the Leukemia and Lymphoma Society. And thanks to Tony Fasciano, Staci Hou, Vanessa Jeong, Kate Kowsh, Chris Stribley, Caroline Maher, Drew Nederpelt, Rachel Trusheim and everyone at Sterling & Ross.

TABLE OF CONTENTS

INTRODUCTION

The stock market crash of 2008 will be remembered for decades to come. It was the year that capitalism failed due to the greed and corruption of the free markets. Our lives will be different going forward, but many lessons were learned about ourselves, including the true amount of risk we all can tolerate.

The first decade in the new millennium will go down as the decade of the bubbles. The run up of technology, housing, financials and commodities created billions of dollars of profit for people around the world, but when the bubbles burst even more money was lost than originally made.

Whether or not the worst is behind us, we will not know until the future. One thing is for certain, the average investor realizes that in order to pick up the pieces and move on, you must go back to the basics.

The intention of this book is to educate you financially so when the next crash arrives, you will hopefully know what to expect and how to properly navigate your investments through the storm.

Sir John Templeton once said, "The four most expensive words in the English language are, 'This time is different.'" Market corrections, economic recessions and depressions will always return. Although each has its special twist, they all have repeatable patterns that can be seen from afar.

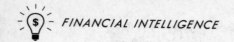

I hope you always remember that the art of investing is not how much money you make when we are living in a bull market; it is how much you can prevent from loss in a bear market.

The lessons and information that can be learned from this book are timeless. By reading this book you will be introduced to the basics of investing as well as the theories and studies that go along with them. I encourage using this book as a reference guide in your everyday investing.

In my opinion, the best strategy for investing is to first know yourself and what you are trying to accomplish. Once you have a firm idea of your intentions, having the financial intelligence of how and where to invest can be instrumental in your long-term success.

TIMELINE OF 2008

JANUARY

2 In the first trading session of 2008, the DJIA falls 220.86 points or 1.7 percent to 13,043.96. This marks the worst drop in a New Year's debut since 1983.

5 The unemployment rate climbs to 5 percent for December, the highest in two years.

8 As bad mortgages and weak consumer spending increase, the DJIA sinks into correction territory, falling 238.42, or 1.9 percent to 12,589.07, down 11 percent from the October 9, 2007 high of 14,164.53.

12 Bank of America buys the largest U.S. mortgage giant, Countrywide Financial for $4 billion.

23 The Federal Reserve lowers the Federal Funds Rate by a half a percent to 3.5 percent.

31 The Federal Reserve lowers the Federal Funds Rate by a half a percent to 3 percent.

FEBRUARY

20 The price of crude oil finishes above $100 a barrel for the first time.

29 The dollar trades at a record low against the euro. The dollar slid 40 percent compared to the euro over the last six years.

MARCH

17 Bear Stearns, an 85-year-old Wall Street titan, nearly collapses before JPMorgan agrees to come to their rescue. The Federal Reserve provides special financing for the rescue, and the original offer is $2 a share, or $236 million. After shareholder opposition, JPMorgan purchases the firm for $10 a share, or $1.4 billion. Just two months earlier, Bear Stearns was trading above $80 a share.

19 The Federal Reserve lowers the Federal Funds Rate by three-quarters of a percent to 2.25 percent.

APRIL

20 New-home sales slide 8.5 percent for March, the lowest since 1991.

MAY

1 The Federal Reserve lowers the Federal Funds Rate by a quarter of a percent to 2 percent.

17 Consumer sentiment about the economy hits a 28-year low.

JUNE

4 Barack Obama wins enough delegates to claim the Democratic presidential nomination.

7 The price of crude oil climbs $11 to finish the day at $138.54 a barrel. The DJIA reacts to increasing oil prices by declining by 394.64 points to 12,209.81. The unemployment rate advances to 5.5 percent; it's the largest one-month gain in 20 years.

9 The average price of gasoline hits $4 a gallon for the first time.

JULY

3 The price of crude oil climbs to $145.29 a barrel. The DJIA officially enters into bear market territory in fear of inflation and rising commodity prices. The DJIA closes down 166.75 points to 11,215.51.

12 IndyMac bank is seized by federal regulators to mark one of the largest bank failures on record.

SEPTEMBER

8 The federal government takes over Fannie Mae and Freddie Mac and promises to buy $1 billion of pre-ferred shares in each.

15 Another Wall Street titan, Lehman Brothers, is forced into liquidation. Bank of America contemplates purchasing Lehman but decides to purchase Merrill Lynch instead.

16 The DJIA reacts to the collapse of Lehman Brothers by falling 504.48 points to 10,917.51, the lowest close in two years. Oil falls below $100 a barrel closing at $95.71 a barrel.

17 The federal government provides AIG an $85 billion bridge loan and temporarily seizes control of the company until the loan is paid off.

30 The House of Representatives votes down the $700 billion rescue package presented by the Bush administration. The DJIA responds by declining 777.68 points or 7 percent, to 10,365.45.

OCTOBER

4 After a revote in the House and then the Senate, President Bush signs the $700 billion plan known as TARP (Troubled Assets Relief Program).

10 The DJIA declines 678.91 points, or 7.3 percent to 8,579.19. After seven straight sessions declines the DJIA is down an additional 20 percent.

11 Marking the "worst week" in 112 years, the DJIA declines an additional 128 points to 8,451.19.

14 The DJIA surges 936.42 points, or 11 percent to 9,387.61, marking its biggest one-day point gain ever.

16 Crude oil falls $4.09 to $74.54 a barrel, down nearly half from its record high.

29 The DJIA surges 889.35 points, or 10.9 percent to 9,065.12, marking its second biggest one-day point gain ever.

30 The Federal Reserve lowers the Federal Funds Rate by a half-point to 1 percent.

NOVEMBER

5 Barack Obama is elected as the 44th President of the United States of America.

6 The DJIA declines 486.01 points to 8,695.79 marking the worst percentage loss ever for the day after a presidential election.

8 The unemployment rate jumps to 6.5 percent, a 14-year high.

20 The DJIA declines 444.99 points to 7,552.29. The S&P 500 index declines to its low from the last bear market.

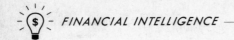

DECEMBER

2 It is announced that the United States economy is in an official recession that began in December of 2007.

12 Former NASDAQ Chairman, Bernard Madoff, is arrested by federal agents for orchestrating a $50 billion Ponzi scheme.

17 The Federal Reserve lowers the Federal Funds Rate to a target range of 0 to 0.25 percent.

19 The 30-year fixed mortgage falls to an average rate of 5.17 percent, its lowest point since 1971 when Freddie Mac began tracking rates.

31 The DJIA finishes at 8,776.39, down 33.8 percent for the year. The year 2008 marks the third worst year ever in the history of the DJIA and the worst since 1931.

CHAPTER 1

WHAT DOES RETIREMENT MEAN TO YOU?

All of us have differing views of what retirement means. To some, it is the ability to not need to work for money. To others, it is the ability to retire comfortably.

Years ago, the hypothetical picture of retirement was painted as such: employees worked their whole life for the same employer, retired with a staff luncheon and a gold watch and wandered into the sunset where they spent the remaining years of their life in a rocking chair on the porch. Unfortunately, this is not that far from an exaggeration of the truth.

Defining Retirement

Retirement is really a passage from one journey to another. To make the most of retirement, you should consider "retiring to something," not "retiring from something." Retirement should represent the next stage of your life. And since this stage can last 30+ years, it is imperative that proper planning starts now to ensure your ultimate dreams come true. Therefore, take the time now to begin your future journey. It is never too early to begin the process.

Unfortunately, it is true what people say. Most people tend to spend more time planning their two-week summer vacation than they do planning for their retirement. The more you determine what you want, the easier and quicker you'll find the path to your retirement years.

How Did it Come to This?

Let's break lifespan into thirds through age 90. The first third of one's life accomplishes very little in proactively planning for retirement. The next third of one's life, the main working years, that worker has double duty. That is, to determine how to save enough money during that 30-year working period to last 60 years! The last third, one is not generating much in the way of new income, yet, that person needs to have sufficient funds on hand to last that final 30-year period. That's a tough one!

Some people state that the government will take care of older Americans during retirement through Social Security. Well, not really. In fact, Social Security was designed to be a supplement to an existing retirement plan set up and already provided for by an employer, with the balance generated through savings. Unfortunately, it really hasn't worked out that way. This is something we need to come to grips with and plan accordingly for since the retired investor has less room for unfavorable changes than a worker. As a worker, if the numbers don't work according to plan, you have options. You can work longer, save more, spend less during your working years or perhaps change your tolerance for risk. As a retired worker, you're at the mercy of the financial times that lie ahead with little room for error.

Six Critical Issues You Face During Retirement

To begin thinking about this, you must answer tough questions as they relate to the following: longevity, running out of money, inflation, income, volatile stock market and estate issues.

How Long Your Retirement Will Last: Longevity

The life span of the typical American has increased dramatically over the past few decades, largely as a result of advances in health care and nutrition. Years ago, the length of time one spent in retirement was minimal because people did not have the longevity that they do today. Today, people are living longer than ever before.

In fact, spending one-third of your lifetime in retirement is not uncommon. So now, the challenge is to plan not just to retirement but through retirement. This makes it more difficult since this was not what we had in mind when we first decided to put away funds for retirement.

Take these facts: According to the U.S. Department of Health and Human Services, in 1900, a 65-year-old American had an average life expectancy of 1.2 additional years, today a 65-year-old man has a life expectancy of 15.3 years and a 65-year-old woman has an average life expectancy of 19.1 years. To put it in a different perspective, the average 65-year-old has a 56 percent chance of living to age 80, and a 36 percent chance of living to age 85. These facts present challenges that are both good news and bad news. The good news is that a longer life span will enable you to accomplish more of what you have been dreaming about. The bad news is that you need to be financially capable of making that happen! Longer life spans require greater financial resources, since the costs of medical care, nursing home care, hospice care and the like escalate to dollar amounts unimaginable in years past.

Running Out of Money Before You Run Out of Time

Because of this increased longevity, running out of money represents your biggest challenge. This problem occurs more often than you think. Many older individuals will outlive their savings and will be forced to live on amounts provided by the government and/or their employer, such as Social Security and possibly an employee pension. People aged 85 and above are twice as likely to be living under the poverty level as those between the ages of 65 and 74.

Most of us tend to underestimate how much time we have and overestimate the amount of money we will have to safely spend during retirement. This will result in not having sufficient funds to last during retirement.

How Much Your Living Expenses Increase Over Time: Inflation

You'll need to prepare for the challenge of inflation.

Inflation addresses the issue that $1 saved today does not equal $1 called upon in the future—when we need those funds. Historically, inflation has averaged 3.1 percent per year since 1926. Of even greater uncertainty is the fear of the unknown that could have a devastating effect on your resources. Just look at the late '70s and early '80s when inflation averaged double digits for many years. The unpredictability of future living costs poses significant challenges and complications during the planning process.

Income

How much income is really enough? Can you really oversave? Can you outlive your income? These are tough questions, with no easy answers. The good news is that people tend to need less money to live on during their golden years. A good rule of thumb is that people tend to spend approximately 80 percent of their current living expenses during retirement. Another way of saying the same thing is that retirees need about 80 percent of their income (before tax) earned in the final working years. However, as with any rule of thumb, it is not a one size fits all solution. The amount you accumulate will be specific to your needs.

The actual level of income you will need during retirement will depend on many variables. These could include your income before retirement, your age, your health and your newfound lifestyle. You could be spending more money instead of less. Changing habits and patterns of retirees will dictate most of what is yet to come. Therefore, plan on spending more than you probably would.

Volatile Stock Market

What happens if you were planning on beginning your retirement during an unfortunate period? For example, suppose you were to begin retirement during the latter half of 2008 with a stock market that has not seen the likes of such volatility since the Great Depression! Most of us assume we will have a certain amount of money available at retirement, but that may not always be the case. The latter half of 2008 definitely threw most of us for a loop! Therefore, having a proper allocation of investments will help us (but not provide an absolute fix) in going a long way.

Estate Planning: How Much Will You Leave Behind for Your Heirs?

Leaving assets to your heirs will also dictate what you can afford to spend during retirement. Because most retirees will need to draw on their accumulated savings and investments, their desire to leave behind an estate for their children or other family members, and provide gifts to religious institutions or other favorite charities, pose a direct conflict with their retirement objectives.

What you will find is that you can't have your cake and eat it too! With a limited amount of financial resources, care must be taken in determining what you can spend on yourself and family members during retirement versus what can be given away or left behind to others. This is a decision you alone are faced with.

As you can see, the challenges we face can be daunting. Proper planning and a desire to take charge of your own financial intelligence can go a long way in being prepared for the inevitable, especially with the current finanicial uncertainty in which we all live.

Five Common Retirement Planning Mistakes People Make

Now that we know what challenges lie ahead, we need to do everything we can to address them intelligently. Unfortunately, too many of us don't do the little things we should in helping us get to our chosen destination. And while we were able to achieve success before retirement, the challenges we face during retirement can be beyond our control. The following is a brief explanation of some of the mistakes we make when planning our own retirement.

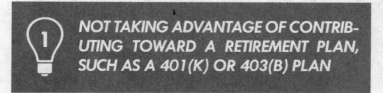

1 NOT TAKING ADVANTAGE OF CONTRIBUTING TOWARD A RETIREMENT PLAN, SUCH AS A 401(K) OR 403(B) PLAN

As they say, there is no time like the present to begin saving! Max out your account if you can. This is one of the few remaining pre-tax benefits you can get since it is a direct offset against your total W-2 (wage) income. So not only can you reduce your taxable income each year, you will see the overall effects of compounding your annual investment. For example, look at the effect of compounding by maxing out your 401(k) in the following situations:

Age	Annual Savings	Growth Rate	Future Value at age 65
25	$16,000*	8%	$4,144,904
35	$16,000*	8%	$1,812,531
45	$16,000*	8%	$732,191
55	$16,000*	8%	$231,785

* Note that the max 401(k) contribution can change every year so that maxing out your 401(k) should result in you putting away more than the stated number above.

Furthermore, if your employer matches some or all of your contribution, the increase in your account can be astronomical.

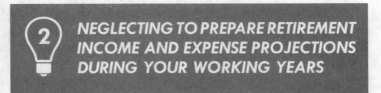

2 NEGLECTING TO PREPARE RETIREMENT INCOME AND EXPENSE PROJECTIONS DURING YOUR WORKING YEARS

This is critical; otherwise, you won't know whether you will save enough to cover expenses during retirement. I'll show you an easy chart I use that can help you gain control over the situation.

The beginning balance is the money you have accumulated during your working years. Additions represent things like pensions, Social Security, other income and investment income. Withdrawals include things like basic and discretionary expenses and taxes. The beginning balance plus additions less withdrawals gives you the ending balance.

The ending balance is the beginning balance for the following year. If these balances decline to zero at an age earlier than your life expectancy, then you need to rethink your long-term retirement strategy. I'm using a hypothetical example as an example of the way you should set this up. You can see that this hypothetical investor will run out of money at age 72.

Age	Beginning Balance	+ Additions	- Withdrawals	= Ending Balance
65	$500,000	$50,000	$100,000	$450,000
66	$450,000	$55,000	$110,000	$395,000
67	$395,000	$60,000	$120,000	$335,000
68	$335,000	$65,000	$130,000	$270,000
69	$270,000	$70,000	$140,000	$200,000
70	$200,000	$75,000	$150,000	$125,000
71	$125,000	$80,000	$160,000	$45,000
72	$45,000	$85,000	$130,000	$0

3 EXPECTING SOCIAL SECURITY TO COVER ALL YOUR NEEDS AT RETIREMENT

Social Security was created as part of FDR's New Deal and instituted in 1937. Its purpose was to supplement a worker's retirement at age 65, which was supposed to be primarily funded with employer retirement dollars, such as defined benefit plans. Unfortunately, too many people believe that is still the case and are disenchanted when they don't have the funds necessary to retire in the manner they would like.

There is also the thought that Social Security won't even be there when you are ready to collect. I wouldn't be too concerned with that. It will be there in some way, shape or form, but may not be recognizable as it is today. It is too popular a program for the government to disband. Furthermore, it would be political suicide for any elected official to even present that option. It could be subject to a needs test or some other discriminatory factor. The bottom line is this: don't rely on someone else or some other entity to fund your own retirement. Do it yourself!

4 ACCEPTING AN EARLY RETIREMENT OFFER FROM YOUR EMPLOYER WITHOUT THINKING IT THROUGH

All too often, people can't wait to leave their jobs. The

fact that the employer will front-load money is even that much more of a bonus. Many people do not make the proper calculations to determine whether the money will be sufficient to retire on, or if it should be used as a partial retirement amount if they have a desire to go back to work. For example, let's say you are at the age of 55, and wish to accept your employer's early retirement offer. Assuming your salary is $80,000 per year, and you were getting 5 percent annual pay increases, and you anticipated working another 10 years, here's how the numbers would look:

> $80,000 Payment (PMT)
> 10 more years till regular retirement (N)
> 5 percent growth rate for pay raises (I)
> Present Value (PV) = $617,739

Translation: You need to receive a retirement package of at least $617,739 (not counting insurance and other fringe benefits you currently receive) to equal the payout you would get over the next 10 years! I would venture to say that most people never look that far and receive a fraction of this amount.

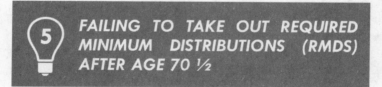

5 **FAILING TO TAKE OUT REQUIRED MINIMUM DISTRIBUTIONS (RMDS) AFTER AGE 70 ½**

With the exception of 2009 only, individuals are required to take out a required minimum distribution (RMD) from their retirement account by April 1st in the year in which they turn 70 ½. Failure to do so will result in a penalty of 50 percent of the excess distribution that should have come out. Since this distribution represents income (not previously taxed at an earlier date during your working years), you must add this amount to all your other income streams. And since it is taxed at ordinary income rates, it can push you into a higher income tax bracket.

How Much Income are You Likely to Need from Your Personal Investments?

Based on the above scenarios, maxing out our retirement investment income can be a struggle. We now have to weigh all these factors together and determine an overall game plan on how to tackle this issue. Much of how you proceed will be determined through the amount of risk you are willing to take, your time horizon until retirement, how liquid and marketable you want your funds to be, the income tax consequences of your actions, and by providing a properly diversified portfolio to weather out the unforeseen storms.

Summary

Now that you have seen all the issues involved in preparing for retirement, there is no substitute for an acceptable financial plan to cover all of these basics. It's like a financial roadmap. You have a destination, but want specific guidance on how to get there. Just picture yourself driving from NYC to LA. You know you have to go west, but a road map pointing out which roads to take make the journey that much easier.

Therefore, changing the game plan mid-stream to work through the facts above presents a tough scenario and may not be able to be accomplished without proper planning and guidance going forward. The one common denominator that links all of these thoughts together is your ability to become independently wealthy and provide the freedom for you to choose retirement on your own terms. That's what this book is all about. Achieving financial intelligence will guide you toward making these smooth and successful decisions. The balance of this book will provide that financial roadmap to you to help you discover your own "financial intelligence."

CHAPTER 2

HOW TO PREPARE FOR A SUCCESSFUL RETIREMENT

How Do You Begin?

Now that I have shown you what you need to be concerned about, let's start planning! You will need to develop a financial plan. As stated earlier, a financial plan provides the financial roadmap for this long and strenuous journey. The following are the seven steps in the financial planning process.

The Financial Planning Process

1. Gather all necessary data.

2. Objectives need to be set.

3. Budget yourself.

4. Process all info into meaningful personal financial statements.

5. Develop a long-term plan.

6. Implement those recommendations.

7. Monitor your situation annually.

GATHER ALL NECESSARY DATA

There are two types of data necessary to gather. We'll call it "quantitative" and "qualitative." Quantitative data are the hard facts that you see when reviewing your financial statements and much more. Examples of quantitative information include your last three years of tax returns (that's because you can go back and amend up to three years), your estate planning documents (including wills, deeds, trust documents, living wills, powers of attorneys, etc.), your before tax information (retirement plans and employee benefit information), your after-tax investments (such as dollar cost averaging, and other routine or monthly investments), your charitable gifting strategies, your education accounts, your business documents (including buy-sell agreements and other instruments if you have partners) and other documents where amounts can be pulled from. Remember, the more information you accumulate, the better! This will ensure that you have taken into account as much critical information as necessary. You can never have enough information. That's because your plan will be more representative of what you own.

 ## OBJECTIVES NEED TO BE SET

There is a clear distinction between goals and objectives. Goals are open-ended broad statements. For example, you may have a goal that you want to be rich! The problem with that goal is how do you define rich? Rich can mean different things to different people. Furthermore, it may have or not have a monetary value. Is it retiring at age 60 on $2 million or retiring at age 55 on $200,000 of income per year? Therefore, objectives are both definite and measurable. There is a definite time frame and dollar amount tied to each objective. And what we are going to learn is that each objective will have a distinct investment(s) tied to it. Therefore, some objectives with shorter time frames may have an entirely different investment philosophy than other objectives which have a longer time horizon.

Prioritize your objectives. That means list your most important ones first and so forth. That's because you will have many objectives and limited resources. And because you will not be able to achieve all the objectives you have listed, make your resources count!

 3   **BUDGET YOURSELF**

Budgeting is critical to managing your daily financial operations. With budgeting, your purpose is to:

- Set a forecasted amount for each revenue and expense item.

- Identify variances between actual and budgeted numbers.

- Define possible problems in spending patterns.

- Identify opportunities to overcome these problems.

- Help you realistically plan to improve your spending patterns.

Your budget should carefully balance the various needs of all your family members. Perhaps setting up a personal allowance for each family member can get the job done. When preparing your own budget reconciliation, remember to leave a comfortable margin for discrepancies in your budgeted numbers and for those unexpected expenses that were not even considered in the first place.

Consider the following tips when developing your budget:

<u>Design a budget that is suitable for you</u>. Budgets come in a variety of formats. You can even use a computerized version through one of the many software vendors available. Some of these programs are integrated with other types of software, such as tax software.

<u>Forecast your income</u>. Be realistic in estimating your income, and particularly nonrecurring items (income that is not received on a regular basis). Categorize your income. Be conservative when you estimate—or in other words, estimate on the low side.

<u>Summarize past expenses</u>. Past expenses need to be summarized before you can estimate what your future expenses will look like. Categorize these expenses. Take your time when doing this. Ways you can accomplish this include examining past checks, credit card statements and just making a list of all cash expenses. Carry a notepad and pencil and every time you make a purchase, record it. You'll be surprised at how quickly those amounts grow. And after analyzing this, you may conclude that most of these purchases were indeed "impulse" purchases that you probably could have done without.

Estimate future expenses. Now that you have forecasted income and examined past expenses, extend these numbers on a monthly basis and go 12 months out. Again categorize these expenses. Your objective is to budget these future expenses so they don't exceed your income going forward. Your long-term solution will be to minimize your expenses and transfer the excess income amounts into savings. The only caution you should be aware of are nonrecurring expenses (those that don't occur on a monthly basis). These can present a problem when budgeting. Examples of these types of expenses include insurance premiums (which are paid six months or a year in advance), IRA contributions and vacations. Take a monthly estimate and factor that into the budgeting process. Put this money away in advance and when these payments come due, just dip into the account that has been housing these future expenses.

PROCESS ALL INFO INTO MEANINGFUL PERSONAL FINANCIAL STATEMENTS

Now that you have gathered all types of data necessary and prioritized your objectives, you need to take that information and incorporate it into meaningful personal financial statements. The statements you should be developing to tie all your financial information together are the balance sheet and the cash flow statement. These statements show an individual's financial well-being.

The balance sheet. A balance sheet represents a financial snapshot in time. It determines your net worth by showing all your assets and liabilities as of today. Assets are things you own and liabilities are amounts you owe. Assets are recorded at their fair market value (what they are worth today, not what you paid for them). Liabilities are the face amount of the balance owed (the current amount due which is equal to the difference between the original loan and what was paid off against the loan).

Net worth results from the excess equity you own and is determined by taking your assets and subtracting your liabilities. When preparing these statements, try to be as realistic as you can. Value your assets at what you would likely get if you were to sell these assets today. All too often, people tend to overvalue what their assets are really worth. Liabilities are not an issue because it is the amount owed as of a certain valuation date. Also, beware, there will probably be income tax consequences when you do finally sell these assets on the appreciated value.

Once you have an up-to-date personal balance sheet, you should have a better understanding of your current financial situation. Now that you understand what you have as to what you will need over time, you can start planning intelligently as how to increase your net worth. If you are new to your career, don't be discouraged if your numbers are not where you want them to be, such as a low net worth or even a negative one! The important thing is to use your financial intelligence to improve upon it. Periodically checking your net worth helps determine the progress you have made in the financial planning process.

The cash flow statement. The cash flow statement represents all your inflows and outflows that occur during set time intervals. These intervals can range from annual, semiannual, quarterly, monthly or even weekly statements. If you pay all your bills in full, then your inflows will always equal your outflows. If you leave balances on your credit cards, then your outflows will exceed your inflows. This is your true gauge that will show you how much money you are saving. The objective here is to minimize your expenses against your income and take that difference and use it to fund your specific stated objectives that you have identified as discussed previously (i.e. save money for your life goals).

Inflows represent all income items, such as wages, self-employment income, interest, dividends, capital gains, rents, royalties, alimony and other forms of income. Outflows can be broken down into two categories. Fixed outflows are recurring expenses that are fixed in amount and payable monthly or at definitive periods. Fixed expenses include mortgage payments, taxes, insurance payments and other regular expenses. Variable or discretionary expenses are things that you can control, and things that you should try to minimize in order to improve your savings. These expenses include items such as vacations, entertainment and dining, etc.

⑤ DEVELOP A LONG-TERM PLAN

Now that you have reviewed your personal financial statements, you understand what your available resources are. And having prioritized your objectives in life, you should be able to develop a long-term plan that will aid you in your quest for financial security.

Your long-term plan must be specific. That means a dollar amount and time frame must accompany each other. You must have a specific action or step for every item in your plan. Categorize each item by discipline.

- Cash Flow and Budgeting.
- Insurance.
- Investments.
- College Education.
- Income Tax.
- Retirement and Employee Benefits.
- Estate.
- Charitable Giving.

6   IMPLEMENT THOSE RECOMMENDATIONS

This is your "action" or "to-do" list.

Prioritize each category by date so you take care of the most important ones first. I would then list the person responsible. Will it be you, your spouse, the attorney (estate planning), the CPA (for income tax planning), the insurance agent (insurance planning), the investment planning professional (investment planning) or someone else?

The importance of the implementation list and delegating responsibility to the appropriate party is to make sure those things do in fact happen and setting up the road map will ensure their deliverance. These moves are critical because they will help move you along the journey from point A to point B.

I would set it up in the following manner using the following as sample items. I will base the list on the assumption that the current date is 6/30/09:

Implementation: "To-Do" List

RECOMMENDATION	PERSON RESPONSIBLE	DATE DUE
Cash Flow Planning Reduce variable expenses by 10 percent	Husband	7/15/09
Insurance Planning Adjust liability limits for homeowners and automobile policy to the same limit	Insurance Agent	8/1/09
Investment Planning Amend last year's tax return	CPA	9/1/09
College Education Planning Start 529 savings plan	Financial Advisor	9/15/09
Retirement Planning and Employee Benefit Planning Max out 401(k) contribution	Wife	9/15/09
Estate Planning Revise wills	Attorney	10/1/09
Charitable Giving Contact alma mater to set up a charitable trust	Husband	1/1/10

⑦ MONITOR YOUR SITUATION ANNUALLY

Things change! Not only can your personal situation change but also the economic conditions in which the plan was created may change as well. The purpose of the personal financial plan is to ensure that you stay the course. When things move off the roadmap for whatever reason, having this monitoring process in place ensures that you get back on track as quickly and easily as possible.

For your personal situation, when you were devising your initial plan, you were at a certain point in time and the plan you chose was representative of those things important to you in your life. However, life evolves and things could change. For example, you may have gotten married, had children, been divorced, received a raise, changed or lost jobs, moved to the suburbs, bought a dog or an SUV, etc. You see where this is going. None of these things were relevant at the time the plan was made so the plan needs to be monitored so it can change.

Or the economic scenario could change (just turn on CNN). Imagine if you were creating your first plan in the late '70s. Much was going on then. We had double digit inflation, double digit interest rates and a poor stock market. Imagine if you ran inflation numbers at 12 percent, when historically they have averaged 3.1 percent over the last 80 years. Your numbers would be far off. And even though minimal change is required when the economy falters, (like the latter half of 2008), you need to design a plan that weathers the course in all financial situations.

Understanding Retirement

So after evaluating your financial well-being, how do you stack up in comparison to the bigger scheme of things? Well, one of the more frequent questions that I am always asked is, "Where should I be in saving for retirement at various ages?" The following is a chart that answers this question, as well as something that will give you a rough road map and understanding of the years ahead.

Where Should You Be in the Retirement Cycle?

Ages 20-29 and 30-39:

- Have an emergency fund equal to six months of gross living expenses.
- Make sure you always have adequate and continuous insurance coverage for life, disability, health, homeowners, automobile and umbrella.
- Purchase your first home. Be careful not to bite off more than you can chew.
- Be careful if moving between jobs and short-changing your pension benefits or other deferred compensation arrangements.
- Roll over any retirement benefits into an IRA or to your next 401(k).
- Minimize your income tax bite by maxing out your deductions.

- Contribute regularly to your 401(k) and/or IRA, and any other retirement fund.
- Write a will.

40-49:
- Contribute regularly to your 401(k) and/or IRA, and any other retirement fund.
- Check your Social Security statement annually to ensure that all your wages have been credited correctly. If not, contact them immediately.
- Analyze personal assets, and work out a plan for funding an adequate retirement income.
- Actively manage your IRA and other retirement funds with appropriate emphasis on capital gains oriented investments.
- Review your will every three years or when moving to another state. Review it with an experienced attorney.

50-59:
- Contribute regularly to your 401(k) and/or IRA, and any other retirement fund.
- Check your Social Security statement annually to ensure that all your wages have been credited correctly. If not, contact them immediately.
- Analyze personal assets, and work out a plan for funding an adequate retirement income.
- Review your retirement income and expense projections taking inflation into consideration.

- Confirm the beneficiary designations on life insurance policies, annuities and retirement plans.
- Join AARP (American Association of Retired Persons).
- Review your will every three years or when moving to another state. Review it with an experienced attorney.

60-66:
- Collect the documents necessary to process Social Security benefits.
- Determine whether it makes sense to sell your primary residence and take the tax consequences into effect.
- Prepare detailed cash flow projections from estimated year of retirement until age 90, taking inflation into consideration.
- Practice living for a month under your new retirement income.
- Determine the status and duration of ongoing loans and mortgage commitments.
- Determine which activities will keep you active during retirement.
- Consider different retirement locations.
- Inquire about possible retirement entitlements from previous employers.
- Consider long-term care insurance.

CHAPTER 3

PLANNING FOR THE GAME OF LIFE

As an overview for what's to come, I have provided you with some general thoughts on how to plan for the "game of life." Different stages of life require different actions to be taken. Furthermore, not everyone's situation will be the same. Therefore, you must plan accordingly.

Life events, as they occur, will awaken you and help you prepare toward the self-realization of your goals and objectives. Some of these events are pre-planned to a certain degree, i.e., taking your first job, getting married or starting a family and some of them are unforeseen events, such as losing a job, getting divorced or becoming widowed. Many of these financial uncertainties become realities at some point during your lifetime. In fact, individuals typically experience at least eight special situations during their lifetime. The former tend to be welcome occurrences. The latter inflicts panic.

You must first identify the particular stage in which you currently stand in life's time horizon. This self-awareness can prepare you for possible changes in your financial planning. Some issues will receive more weight than others. Some of these circumstances will dramatically alter your planning, while others will require minor modifications. Age may play a role in a particular life event. This is an important concept since the American population is getting older. Whether it's a single issue or multiple issues, you may wish to take the precautionary route and develop a comprehensive financial plan to help integrate all pieces of the puzzle.

A complete financial plan comprises all aspects of your financial position and helps create a financial "roadmap" to help you organize your goals in a logical format and attempt to pave the way toward a sound course during your lifetime. Several integrated and coordinated financial planning strategies may be utilized toward fulfilling those needs and goals. Financial life strategies also involve making dollar trade-offs. A sufficient level of spending and saving is necessary when planning the major events of one's lifetime. Making money trade-offs without a financial roadmap may leave you out of gas and far short of the ultimate destination. With this in mind, it becomes necessary to examine whether you're on track at a particular stage within your life cycle. In life cycle planning, you should focus not so much on age, but rather, on the events that have financial significance during one's life. To assist you in helping plan for the unknown, here are some of the important issues that may arise in life's great cycle of events.

Planning for the Seasons of Life

If you are beginning a career, get your finances immediately in order. Avoid the pitfalls of excessive credit card spending. Begin repayment of student loans and develop a budget. Surplus funds should be invested into a regular savings program. Savings should be 10 percent of gross income. Anticipate life's contingencies by establishing an emergency fund, which should consist of six month's worth of living expenses. Design an investment portfolio with properly diversified investments. Don't skip out on needed health insurance and a renter's insurance policy, if applicable.

If you are single, you probably have no one to count on other than yourself. You need to create your own safety net for the long term. Analyze insurances. Health and disability are primary. Life insurance may not be needed if there are no dependents. In case of illness or incompetence, a health care proxy will assist in making decisions and a durable power of attorney or a revocable living trust will help in case you are unable to run your own affairs. Consider choosing an institution, such as a bank or trust company, to share the responsibility with a friend or relative.

If you are married early on in life, you are in an enviable financial position. Much of the financial groundwork begins to take shape. If you and your spouse are working, start a joint savings plan. This includes contributing to retirement accounts, flexible spending accounts and creating an investment portfolio. The approximate cost and date of retirement can be estimated affording you plenty of time to get ready. Since life is unpredictable, it is necessary to seek risk protection. Auto, health and disability insurance should be purchased. You should also change the following beneficiaries: pension plans, IRAs, annuities and living trusts.

If you are buying a home, a significant amount of debt is incurred since the home is usually the biggest purchase an individual makes. Spend time getting to know the neighborhood. Comparison shop for mortgage deals. Purchase homeowners insurance with replacement cost for both dwelling and contents and umbrella insurance to protect the homeowner in the event of future liability claims.

If you are starting a family, life insurance needs to be purchased. The financial impact on your family upon premature death can be overwhelming. Revise the will once your child is born and begin thinking about college funding. College costs have been increasing at a higher rate than inflation. Parents and college-bound children need to learn about new possibilities for college funds and become acquainted with the financial aid process.

If you have young children, a savings program for college is crucial, even if the amount put away each year cannot actually meet projected college costs. You can always finance college through loans, but you can never finance retirement. Put money away for the kids, but not so much that you put your retirement on hold. If you have children closer to college age, evaluate your current financial position in order to assess what resources, if any, might be used to fund college costs. When the children are young, estimate the amount of money needed to pay tuition bills and the dates when these bills will arrive.

If your kids have graduated college and are out of the house, your prime earning years are probably approaching. If you have not already done so, saving for retirement should become a standard requirement and an automatic deduction from salary. Maximize contributions to 401(k) plans, 403(b) plans, Keogh plans and other types of deferred savings vehicles. You can always do an IRA if you have earned income.

You may elect to downgrade your house to a smaller residence. If you have lived in the house for at least two of the past five years, you can exclude up to $250,000 if you are single or up to $500,000 if you are married. If you lived in the house for less than that, and had to move for what is deemed an unforeseen circumstance, then you may be able to prorate that gain. However, don't be too quick to sell. More and more children are moving in with their parents after graduating college.

You need to be really focused during the several years before you approach retirement. Continue with a similar investment strategy to the one you began years before. Don't become too conservative. Don't completely pull out of equities and go into fixed income. Fixed-income accounts may not perform as well as equities over the long haul, because of early retirement trends and increased longevity. Nowadays, it is possible that retirement could total one-third of a person's lifetime. Preserving capital is more important than maximizing return. You should consider formulating an estate plan and have an attorney review all legal documents to ensure that they are in accordance with your goals. "Providing effectively for survivors" means that you must plan as if you were going to die tomorrow, however unlikely that may be.

Planning for Life's Uncertainties

If you are terminated from your job, extreme worry and preoccupation may result. You probably cannot predict how long you will remain unemployed. The main problem will probably be how long you can stretch unemployment income to pay living expenses during unemployment. This can be calculated through the use of a budget.

Assume that you will remain unemployed between six and nine months and apply for unemployment benefits. If a layoff is imminent, seek a severance package and secure good references. One thing that tends to happen is the omission and cancellation of what many people view as unnecessary items to carry and pay for during a prolonged work stoppage. Your insurance needs should never go away so don't make that one of the first items to go. Bottom line, don't forget to continue your insurance coverage.

To counter the immediate urge to sell off investments to foot the bills, develop a cash flow analysis that provides a reasonable idea of how long existing funds will last. This approach will enable you to be calm and orderly when contemplating necessary financial decisions. If the company offers you either a lump sum or a continuation of salary, check the facts. Generally, a lump sum will be better but not always. Before you decide, see if salary continuation will prolong benefits, such as health insurance and funding of a retirement plan. If so, salary continuation will be a better deal.

If you are getting a divorce, create a team of specialized professionals to help structure the divorce settlement which could have realistic and fair expectations. Find out about the current trends in the way divorce settlements are structured in your state. Mediation may be a less expensive alternative. You will then have to start developing a new plan dealing with all the areas of financial planning.

Income tax decisions may also be a factor. Dependency deductions can prove more beneficial to the spouse with the higher income. Insurance coverage may need to be updated to remove an ex-spouse as beneficiary. Credit must now be reestablished by the spouse who had no previous credit history and an adjustment to your changed financial status may become a rude awakening.

If you get married after divorce, the question becomes how can you protect the kids from your first marriage? Look at both family resources and demands for each. Inquire about when the money will be spent. Take a long-term view. Once it is determined what things need to be paid for, you should start investing in order to meet those goals.

To satisfy estate planning needs, set up a qualified terminal interest property (QTIP) trust for the benefit of the spouse. This gives your spouse access to all income for life, but upon death, the assets pass to the intended beneficiaries, usually the children from the prior marriage. If the children are close to the same age, give a portion of the estate to your children at death, with the rest going into a QTIP.

After the death of a spouse, your financial plan may need revisiting. Take it slow. Gather important documents, such as the death certificate, insurance policies and financial account information. An attorney should be contacted. Changing of titles and ownership will need to be performed. Resources must be identified to settle the estate.

If the decedent had life insurance, a choice must be made by the beneficiary as to the disposition of the proceeds. Lump-sum settlements, fixed payments and annuities are three ways to receive these payments. One thing should be avoided: don't feel pressured to spend that money immediately.

Consider taking a lump sum and parking it in treasuries or cash for six months until you get through the hurdle. Credit must be reviewed to ensure that the survivor does not borrow more than he or she should. Assess the composition of your assets, such as investment portfolios, as well as the capability of surviving family members to manage these investments. Stability of income may be something of concern to you. However, don't get too conservative with the remaining investments. The period of widowhood could last as long as 40 years.

Ownership designations on invested assets and disposition of closely held business interests must also be evaluated as well as whether to utilize the marital deduction, any unused unified credit or disclaim the property. A federal estate tax return may need to be filed if the estate has over the threshold for passing assets on to heirs. State tax laws vary. See a CPA or other qualified tax professional to help you sort through the potential mess.

Your income tax filing status will change to widow or widower. However, up to a year after death, as a surviving spouse, you may still file a tax return as married filing jointly and can still claim a dependency exemption for your deceased spouse. If you, as surviving spouse, have children that qualify as dependents, then your home (as a surviving spouse) is your principal residence. If you, as the survivor, provide over half the cost of maintaining your household where your children still live with you, and you have not remarried, then you will be allowed to file a joint return as a surviving spouse for two years after the date of death of your spouse. Retirement projections will have to be revised to account for the changed circumstances.

The most important part of any financial plan involves constant monitoring of life events. It's easy to get off track. Make sure you are logical and rational in your future actions. The bottom line is that you need to make sure that you stay the course.

Take a moment to answer the questions on the following chart to ensure that you have begun planning appropriately.

PLANNING FOR THE GAME OF LIFE:
A Quick Evaluation

Now that you have a brief idea of where you should be in your stage of life, please take a few minutes to complete this checklist. Any "no," "not sure" and even some "yes" answers can point to potential problems you may wish to investigate.

Monthly Income and Expenses

1. Do you use a budget?	Yes	No	Not Sure
2. Have you addressed any financial problems that require immediate attention?	Yes	No	Not Sure

Retirement

1. Are you saving for retirement?	Yes	No	Not Sure
2. Do you know what rate of return you need to maintain your lifestyle and ahead of inflation and taxes?	Yes	No	Not Sure

Children's Education

1. Have you planned for this expense?	Yes	No	Not Sure
2. Is the ownership of your education savings designed to reduce taxes?	Yes	No	Not Sure

Your Investments

1. Are they well diversified?	Yes	No	Not Sure
2. Do you know what rate of return you need to maintain your lifestyle and ahead of inflation and taxes?	Yes	No	Not Sure

Risk and Insurance

1. Will your insurance cover your family's needs in the event of death or disability?	Yes	No	Not Sure
2. Do you have an umbrella liability policy?	Yes	No	Not Sure

Estate Planning

1. Are your wills current?	Yes	No	Not Sure
2. Is your estate designed to minimize taxes and fees?	Yes	No	Not Sure

If you answered "no" or "not sure" to two or more of these questions, you should sit down with your Certified Financial Planner® or Certified Public Accountant (CPA) to figure out where the holes are and how to fill them.

Visit www.jacobgoldbooks.com for a downloadable version of all tables and worksheets.

CHAPTER 4

IT ALL STARTS WITH CASH FLOW

Are you one of those individuals who live paycheck to paycheck? Many people have come to accept it and practice it as a way of life! They know it's not the best way to approach managing their cash, but they do it anyway. Why? Perhaps it's becoming more commonly accepted. Or perhaps it's easier. After all, it is pretty easy to obtain a credit card when the credit card company provides you with a maximum credit limit you would never dream of spending. Essentially, it is too easy to spend!

Perhaps it's a sign of the times. People did not use debt during the Great Depression the way they do today. People simply did not believe in debt back then. Their views were that if they did not have sufficient funds to pay for something, they did without it. When you stop to think about it, they all got by. Maybe we should go back to that mentality and work with the dollars we have on hand.

If we don't change our habits soon, it will affect us in significant ways. And as you have seen over the last year and through one of the worst financial crises ever, living with debt may not be the prudent thing to do going forward. It is important to remember that credit is a privilege, not a right, so you need to make sure that you do not abuse it so it can be there for you when you need it.

Therefore, the lifestyle we choose should be based on available cash. If you make $50,000 per year, then you should spend less than that and keep the balance for savings. That balance will be the key to meeting your long-term objectives.

Choosing your lifestyle is a learned process. It also has adjustments based on whether your income increases or decreases throughout the years. If you are living paycheck to paycheck, then your style of living currently is a little bit above what you earn. While our income typically increases over time, only at that point should our lifestyle increase since we have the funds to justify it. What is critical is that you practice effective cash flow management.

Many individuals underestimate the importance of cash flow management. Effective cash flow management has two primary objectives. The first is to manage income and expenses in order to establish and maintain a reserve of cash or near-cash equivalents to meet unanticipated or emergency needs, including the expenses of sudden illness, injury or death, or as a cushion for possible loss of employment. The second is to create and maintain a systematic surplus of cash (reserve) directed toward specific types of investments for capital accumulation.

Both of these objectives represent an integral and essential part of the personal financial planning process and are a prerequisite to the development of a personal financial plan. Without focusing in these areas, you will find it more difficult to accomplish your goals.

The premise of financial planning is built on cash flow management. It is through this monthly surplus of funds that you can accomplish several financial goals. This surplus of funds will ensure that you have enough cash and other liquid assets to conduct ongoing family operations, to have an adequate emergency fund to meet unforeseen contingencies, to minimize unproductive assets, to prevent illiquidity from becoming a problem, and to earmark toward children's education, retirement and various long-term goals and objectives.

Cash flow management can help you achieve future financial independence. Achievement of this goal requires regular growth of your family's personal net worth. This is accomplished primarily by adding regularly to savings and investment assets out of current net cash flow. If net cash flow is negative or zero instead of positive, net worth will decline or remain constant and you will slip further away from your goals. If this occurs, you may wish to develop a budget.

Cash Flow Analysis

Once you are satisfied with a workable budget, cash flow analysis can then be performed. Cash flow analysis is the gathering of reliable cash inflow and cash outflow information from you, and summarizing that information in the form of a cash flow statement. This will help you determine whether the calculation results in a net positive or negative cash flow. A negative cash flow requires immediate attention and action. Just like big companies, individuals cannot afford or will be unable to go for long periods of time without having available funds. Unfortunately, many individuals are not aware of their spending pattern until they see it analyzed for them in black and white. As a result, this exercise could prove to be a valuable learning tool.

You need to take a realistic estimate of your expected income and expenses. How detailed the income and expense information needs to be depends on your judgment about how much is required to produce an accurate plan that you will be able to maintain. If it is determined during the development of your financial plan that available income is less than the amount required to achieve your financial goals (overall expenses), you will then have to make some adjustments.

The whole secret to performing financial planning the right way is through cash flow analysis. Cash flow analysis really involves two choices you must make with the money you receive. You can either save the money (savings) or spend the money (fixed or discretionary). Ideally, you want to reduce your expenses (you probably have more leeway to reduce discretionary expenses as compared to fixed expenses) and channel that money into savings. The savings amounts are then earmarked toward each of the objectives you have identified for yourself for the long term.

Steps in Cash Flow Analysis

There are three steps you may use in analyzing cash flow. They are:

- Gathering current cash flow data.

- Estimating future income and expenses.

- Creating a cash flow statement.

The first step you should perform is to gather current cash flow data. This involves knowing all sources of cash inflow and all cash outflows. Successful completion of this step will help you develop a complete understanding of where money is coming from and where it is going. It is vital to making decisions about short-term spending priorities and in implementing long-term strategies. A daily log of cash outlays is an appropriate starting point.

When gathering income, you should consider all of the following:

- Explore all possible sources.

- Verify these sources from income tax returns for the past three years.

- Subtotal these amounts for ease of use and subsequently include in a cash flow statement.

When gathering expenses, you should consider the following to establish spending patterns:

- Your checkbook.

- Your charge cards.
- Petty cash.

Expenses should be separated into tax-deductible and non-tax-deductible expenses. These amounts should be entered also in the information questionnaire.

The second step is estimating future income and expenses. When estimating expenses for the short and long term, you should categorize these expenses for control purposes into fixed and discretionary expenses. Fixed expenses are necessities that you have little control over. Examples here would include: rent, mortgage, food, clothing, auto, insurance, utilities, taxes, loans or charge accounts, etc. Savings are next, followed by discretionary expenses. Discretionary expenses are items over which you have a greater degree of control. Discretionary expenses pose the greatest likelihood to be reduced, delayed indefinitely or eliminated, if need be. They tend not to be as critical as fixed expenses.

The projection should be used to help you think through the kinds of living expense changes that may be likely over the next five years. These changes should be quantified and considered against your financial goals. Included in these projections should be references to the inflation rate, income tax rates, salary changes or other areas which may be subject to change.

Living expense changes may include care for aging parents, college expenses, possible new family members or a new car, house or other changes that will have a direct impact on living expenses. The projection will not only help you set current priorities, but will also serve as a motivator in many cases. Further, it will provide a good benchmark for annual review purposes. You may even want to use software for tracking personal spending.

When projecting future expenses, you should also provide for contingencies. Contingency plans refer to the need for you to have an emergency fund or adequate insurance coverage in place. The emergency fund is intended to meet expenses that are not included in the family budget, such as unexpected repairs and maintenance. It also provides living expenses in the event of a job loss or unpaid leave of absence for the income earner. This fund should equal three to six months of expenses and should be invested in a fairly liquid money market type of investment. The accumulation of this fund should be addressed immediately in cash flow planning.

The last step in analyzing cash flow is through the construction of a cash flow statement. The cash flow statement shows the net change in inflows and outflows over time as determined by your receipts and disbursements. Expenses and income are condensed into general categories for comparison purposes. Examples of inflows on the cash flow statement include salary or self-employment income, interest, dividends, net rental income and income tax refunds. Outflows include housing, food, clothing, transportation, insurance, taxes, savings and investments. Analyzing a cash flow statement will help you better understand your spending habits over time as well as identify and achieve your goals. The cash flow statement is in contrast to a balance sheet, which provides you with a "snapshot" or picture at a given point in time and should be updated annually.

Tips for Improving Your Cash Flow

The following are some tips you can use to improve your cash flow:

 1 ORGANIZE YOURSELF BETTER

Try to keep your records, organized, labeled and in the same location. Purchase a file cabinet and keep all your records in it. Organize it in alphabetical order or categorize by group. Develop a system that makes it easier for you to locate these documents when needed.

 2 DEDICATION

Dedicate yourself to tracking your cash flow at least monthly. In the beginning, it may be more frequent than what you ultimately end up doing on a routine basis since it will be a new experience for you and will probably take you a little longer. You will also realize things for the first time that you never knew existed beforehand. Once you work out the kinks, you can operate a very efficient strategy for budgeting and ultimately cash flow management.

3 LEAVE HOME WITH LESS CASH

If you don't have the money to spend, it won't happen. You won't be tempted and you'll show greater fiscal restraint.

4 KILL THE CREDIT CARDS

Everyone should have a credit card or two for emergencies. Don't rely on them as a crutch or until you receive your next paycheck or worse yet, for an impulse purchase. Interest rates on credit cards are exorbitant. Then what happens is that when you purchase too much, you tend to pay off the minimum balance and no progress on paying the debt ever occurs. That debt lingers for a very long time.

5 GIVE YOURSELF & FAMILY MEMBERS A WEEKLY ALLOWANCE

If all family members spend what they have and no more, future problems can be avoided. Perhaps provide an in-

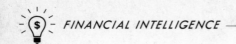

centive to that family member who stays within the budgeted amount the best.

 SET "SAVING" AS A PRIORITY EXPENSE

Savings should come before most other expenses. Unfortunately, certain expenses, like the mortgage, rent, insurance and taxes cannot be avoided. But try to make savings the next big expenditure. As we stated before, you need savings to fund your ultimate long-term objectives.

 REFINANCE YOUR DEBT DURING TIMES OF LOWER INTEREST RATES

It may make sense (though not always) to refinance your home debt, car debt, student loan debt, credit card debt or other outstanding debt especially when interest rates are low. Refinancing this debt can result in lower monthly payment thus freeing up money for you to save for long-term objectives.

 GIVE YOURSELF "INCENTIVES" FOR A JOB WELL DONE

We keep talking about minimizing expenses to help fund long-term objectives. But this requires hard work.

And any time hard work is involved, you should be rewarded for achieving success. Set realistic objectives, try to come in under your budgeted numbers and treat yourself to a little bit (but not a lot) of the savings—as an added incentive. You'll still end up spending less and enjoy some treats not originally earmarked.

Cash Flow Reality

Like a balance sheet, a cash flow statement shouldn't take you more than a few hours to prepare. The better your financial records, the quicker the process will take to complete.

Once you have prepared your first cash flow statement, future ones should not take as long because you will already know how to run the process. Your expense categories will have been identified already, as well as the amounts spent on major items like your mortgage, car payments, insurances, etc. This will make it easier to forecast.

Also remember, that the creation of a cash flow statement in and of itself will not change your financial life. It is not a spending plan. A cash flow statement simply increases awareness of current income and expenses and how those amounts compare.

Once your current cash flow information has been analyzed, summarized, projected and a cash flow statement has been prepared, you are now in a position to perform the next level of service, which is cash flow planning. This step will be accomplished throughout the various areas of financial planning, which are insurance, investments, retirement and income tax; estate and education and will be covered later.

Below is a cash flow statement to help you begin the process.

CASH FLOW STATEMENT

	MONTHLY	ANNUALLY
INCOME		
Your Net (Take-Home) Pay		
Your Spouse's Net (Take-Home) Pay		
Investment Income (Dividends, Interest, Capital Gains)		
Other Income (Rent, Royalties, Social Security)		
TOTAL INCOME		
EXPENSES		
FIXED EXPENSES – HOUSING		
Rent/Mortgage		
Taxes (Property)		
Gas/Electricity		
Fuel (Home Heating)		
Water/Garbage/Sewer		
Telephone		
Household/Yard Maintenance		
Other		
FIXED EXPENSES – GROCERY		
Groceries (Food & Non-Food)		

	MONTHLY	ANNUALLY
Meals Away From Home		
Other		
FIXED EXPENSES – CAR		
Car #1 Payment		
Car #2 Payment		
Fuel		
Maintenance/Repairs		
License(s)		
Carpool/Parking		
Other		
FIXED EXPENSES – PERSONAL		
Family Purchases		
Uniforms/Work Gear		
Dry Cleaning/Laundry		
Toiletries		
Haircuts		
Other		
FIXED EXPENSES – MEDICAL		
Medication(s)		
Medical		
Dental		
Optical		
Other		
FIXED EXPENSES – INSURANCE		
Home/Property		
Auto(s)		
Medical		
Life		
Disability		
Other		
DISCRETIONARY EXPENSES		

	MONTHLY	ANNUALLY
Eating Out		
Memberships		
Vacation/Travel		
Entertainment		
Dependent (Child) Care		
Alimony		
Child Support		
Holiday Gifts		
Charitable Contributions		
Education/School Expenses		
Crafts/Hobbies		
Dues (Union/Professional/Other)		
Newspaper		
Pets (Vet, Meds., Etc.)		
Allowances		
Other		
SAVINGS		
Savings Account/Bonds		
Investments		
IRA/Pension Plan		
Other		
DEBTS		
Miscellaneous		
TOTAL EXPENSES FROM COLUMNS 1 & 2		
SUBTRACT EXPENSES FROM INCOME		
SURPLUS (Deficit)		

CHAPTER 5

DEBT MANAGEMENT: A DIFFICULT TASK

Individuals use extensive amounts of credit to buy almost any conceivable combination of goods and services. The use of credit has become part of our lifestyle, enabling people to enjoy the use of items before they can pay for them outright. However, the use of credit requires committing future income to pay off the debt. As such, the management of debt is an integral part of financial planning that you need to understand.

The increase of debt is a major reason for the low savings rate in the United States. Many consumers carry debt in excess of 20 percent of take-home pay (explained later), which is considered very high. Also, individuals who are subject to unforeseen circumstances, such as a job loss, health issue, etc., are in grave danger of not being able to pay their bills.

Use of debt may be an important tool for you. Debt does have its advantages. For starters, it allows individuals to purchase products on sale, pay for several items together with one check, use goods and services even before they are paid for and avoid laying out money for an employer or others, thus allowing you to be reimbursed before the bill comes through. Borrowing money also helps establish good credit and more favorable terms and rates. In general, debt is best used for large purchases, such as a mortgage for home ownership, where it would be difficult for you to obtain an item for cash.

However, debt does have its disadvantages. Entering into debt (1) requires the payment of interest, which increases the cost of obtaining the item, and (2) entails periodic repayment of principal, which limits funds available for other consumption and savings. Therefore, consumer debt should be avoided as much as possible.

This is particularly true if you are unable to control spending when accumulating consumer debt is readily available. In addition, whereas mortgage interest is deductible for income tax purposes, interest on consumer debt is not. Therefore, any financial benefit of carrying balances on credit cards or financing smaller purchases, such as automobiles, has been reduced. Also, the interest rate you'll pay will be significantly higher than debt secured against your home.

As a rule of thumb, consumer debt repayments (excluding mortgage payments) should be kept below 20 percent of take-home pay. Although 20 percent of take-home pay does not include mortgage or rent payments, it does include all charge card payments as well as auto, personal and student loans. If debt repayments represent 20 percent or more of take-home pay, the debtor is probably stretched to the limit. Debt repayments should be reduced to no more than 15 percent of take-home pay.

Loan officers often use the following rules of thumb in assessing whether a home mortgage will be offered to a prospective borrower.

1. Monthly housing costs (including principal, interest, taxes, fees and insurance) should be no more than 28 percent of the prospective borrower's gross income.

2. Total monthly payment on all debts should be no more than 36 percent of gross monthly income. According to the underwriting guidelines for the Federal National Mortgage Association (Fannie Mae), this includes:

- Monthly housing expenses (including taxes and interest).

- Monthly payments on installment/revolving credit.

- Monthly mortgage payments on non-income producing property.

- Monthly alimony, child support or maintenance payments.

And now with the economy near shambles and companies toughening up credit card borrowing requirements, you should be lower than the above ratios. Really, the best way to approach this is to determine yourself what your comfort level is with respect to debt and ensuring that you have a sufficient amount of money left over to save for those long-term objectives.

Credit Costs

Do you really know what credit costs? You better. There is no such thing as "free" or "cheap" credit. My standing rule is that if it sounds too good to be true, then usually it is. Know what you are paying ahead of time. Shop around lenders. It's no different than shopping for a car, house or other big-ticket item. Fortunately, there are laws that help in this area.

Credit Regulation

The Consumer Credit Protection Act (Truth in Lending) enables you to compare disclosure of credit terms so you can make meaningful comparisons of alternative sources of credit. This law is the cornerstone for Regulation Z of the Federal Reserve System that mandates that the finance charge and the APR be given explicitly to the consumer. The finance charge is the actual dollar amount that the borrower must pay if the loan is given. Costs such as interest and price differential (that is, the difference between the selling price of the item if it is sold on credit and the selling price if it is paid in cash) must be explained to the customer. Items such as points, discounts, service fees, carrying charges and credit insurance must also be explained. The method used to calculate the APR must be disclosed as well.

The cost and payment requirements for different types of consumer credit vary widely. To manage your finances effectively, you must understand the terms of credit as well as its cost.

Types of Consumer Credit

Let's divide consumer credit into several categories:

1. Credit cards.

2. Installment loans.

3. Revolving credit.

4. Bank, finance company and credit union loans.

5. Life insurance loans.

6. Margin account loans.

7. Home equity loans.

Credit Cards

There are three basic types of credit cards: special-purpose cards, travel or entertainment cards and bank credit cards. Among the issuers of special-purpose cards are gasoline, retail store and car rental companies. These cards are usually issued free of charge and can be used only for purchases from the issuing.

The major travel and entertainment cards are American Express and Diners Club. These cards are usually issued for an annual fee of $35 to $600 and can be used around the world. The major bank credit cards, Visa and MasterCard, can be used for travel, entertainment and buying merchandise at stores throughout the world. While travel and entertainment cards make a profit by charging high annual fees to the cardholder and usually somewhat higher charges on the bills submitted by vendors, bank credit card issuers make a profit by:

- Charging high interest rates on unpaid balances.

- Charging modest annual fees for the card.

- Charging participating merchants about 2 to 5 percent of the amount billed.

Another type of card is the debit card, also called a bank card or cash card. Although it looks like a credit card, the debit card is not used to obtain credit. A debit card is used to pay for a purchase at the time of the transaction. With a debit card issued by a gasoline company, one can buy gasoline, present his or her card for payment, and the system would immediately transfer the money from the cardholder's bank account to the account of the merchant.

If a credit card is lost or stolen, or if the card number is used fraudulently, the owner of the card could be liable for up to $50 of the unauthorized purchases. This $50 liability limit applies if the credit card company is not notified within two business days. There is no liability on the cardholder's part if the credit card company is notified in time or if the card does not provide a place for the cardholder's signature.

Basic safeguards concerning credit cards include keeping a list of credit cards, their numbers and where to call and write in a separate place in case the cards are lost or stolen. The monthly bills should be checked against the customer receipts to ensure that there are no billing errors. Those receipts can also be used to keep track of tax-deductible business or professional expenses.

Installment Loans on Purchases

Installment loans made by banks, finance companies and retailers amortize the principal rather than just require a minimum payment like many credit cards do. Each payment includes a portion of principal repayment as well as an interest payment. The length of installment loans ranges from 12 months to as many as 72 months on some auto loans, with a down payment generally required.

For the borrower, the two key features of an installment loan are:

1. The amount of the monthly payment relative to one's budget.

2. The APR, which must be disclosed to the borrower.

Revolving Credit

In some industries, merchants establish a line of credit with customers. This enables customers to charge purchases up to a specified limit with the privilege of charging additional purchases up to that limit, time and time again, as the balance is reduced.

Bank, Finance Company and Credit Union Borrowing

Most banks and other financial institutions make two other types of personal loans: secured and unsecured. In total cost to you, the secured loan is the more advantageous of the two. The interest rate and the cash outflow requirements are less, and the conditions are not as stringent. Unsecured personal loans are also available, but the APR is usually two percentage points higher than a secured loan.

Life Insurance Loans

Anyone owning a whole life insurance policy that has been in effect for a number of years may obtain a personal loan against the cash surrender value of that policy. As the age of the life insurance policy increases, the amount of money that can be borrowed also increases. The amount that can be borrowed is usually shown in a table that is part of the life insurance policy. The interest rate is also stated and is usually a fixed rate that is quite low. While a life insurance loan is interest-bearing, unpaid interest is added to the loan. This reduces the ultimate life insurance benefit but may offer an attractive current cash flow alternative. In fact, this may be the lowest cost method of obtaining a personal loan.

Life insurance loans are almost automatic. One merely has to inform the insurance company that he or she wants to borrow a certain amount. The company does not need to perform a credit investigation since it has almost perfect collateral. Also, it is not concerned with how the money is used.

Home Equity Loans

Banks have been encouraging consumers to take out home equity loans (in effect, second mortgages) to finance big-ticket items or for home improvements. But be careful. Too much borrowing, again, can cause you problems over the long term. The interest on home equity loans is fully tax-deductible (for those who itemize) as long as the total amount borrowed on first and second mortgages to finance the purchase price of the home or improvements to it is less than $1,000,000.

If the home equity loan is not used for purchase or improvement of the home, the deductibility of the interest is limited to the interest applied to $100,000. Because consumer loan interest lost its deductibility, home equity loans have become more popular. The interest rate is generally lower than consumer debt interest. Since the repayment periods are substantially longer than for most consumer loans, the monthly payments are lower.

When evaluating whether a home equity loan is a suitable vehicle, consider the following:

1.   Is there a cap on the floating interest rate? If so, what is it?

2. What are the origination fees on the loan? Points and closing costs can run into hundreds of dollars.

3. Is the individual endangering the equity in the home if illness or other hardship makes it difficult to continue the payments on both first and second mortgages? The risk of payment default and foreclosure should encourage you to keep home

equity loan payments in line with the consumer debt guidelines.

Credit Life Insurance

Many loans have a provision that provides for credit life insurance or credit disability insurance. The purpose of such insurance is to protect both buyer and lender should the buyer die or become disabled and unable to meet the payments on the loan. The lender receives payment of the balance due on the loan, and the buyer doesn't have to give up the asset that was bought on credit.

Debt Management Tips

1. Don't go crazy. "Debtors Gone Wild" is not a fun exercise and will get you in the poorhouse. Work within the budget rules that we discussed in the last chapter. Limit credit card purchases to what you can really afford to pay.

2. Shop around. Shopping around will help you set your own terms to what works and doesn't work for you. If the terms are not acceptable to you, then look around and find a company whose terms do work for you.

3. Review credit card bills. It happens. Credit card companies do make errors.

DEBT SOLVENCY WORKSHEET
10 Basic Questions

Take this quick 10-question survey to help you manage your debt.

1. Is more than 20 percent of your take-home salary used for credit card payments? Yes No

2. Are you charging more each month than you are paying off? Yes No

3. Have you received calls from credit card companies because of paying bills late? Yes No

4. Do you charge things impulsively? Yes No

5. Are you approaching the limit on your charge cards? Yes No

6. Do you find yourself paying only the minimum payments on your charge cards? Yes No

7. Have you defaulted on a mortgage or rent payment more than once? Yes No

8. Are you uncertain about how much money you owe? Yes No

9. Are you using the cash advance on one credit card to pay off another card? Yes No

10. Is the balance in your savings account shrinking? Yes No

CHAPTER 6

INSURANCE PLANNING ESSENTIALS: PROTECTING YOUR FINANCIAL ASSETS

Insurance is the most important financial discipline. And that's because if your insurance needs are not taken care of properly, then all your other financial disciplines cannot be done right. For example, if your house burns down and you have no homeowners insurance, you will need to raise sufficient funds to find a place to live. You may have to borrow money from investment accounts, like 401(k) plans, brokerage accounts, college funds or any other places you can obtain the necessary funds.

Insurance is kind of an ironic type of investment. Think about it. You are purchasing a product you hope you never have to use. In this situation, you may think you have wasted a significant amount of premium dollars. But the real risk is not having proper coverage.

Risk management issues are present throughout our lives and their maintenance should be a key concern to everyone. Because people don't like talking about insurance, many smart people just ignore the risks inherent in everyday life assuming that nothing bad will ever happen to them. The reality is bad things do happen to good people. As a young teenager I became an Eagle Scout. The Boy Scouts of America taught me something that always stuck with me; you must always be prepared. Preparation comes through the purchase of adequate insurance coverage.

Have You Reviewed Your Insurance Needs Lately?

Even a well thought out financial plan can be ruined if you fail to take the proper precautions to protect your assets. That's where insurance planning comes in. Buying insurance may seem like putting money into something you'll never use. If you're lucky, this will indeed be the case. Unfortunately, you have no way of knowing if you're ever going to use that insurance. All you can do is prepare so that, if an unfortunate event does occur, you and your family will be covered. Being properly and adequately insured can mean the difference between financial security and financial devastation.

What Types of Insurance Do You Need?

Many types of insurance are available today. However, not every kind of insurance is right for everyone. There are probably some types of insurance that you don't need at all. It's also possible that there are some types of insurance that you don't have, but should consider. Once you've carefully reviewed your policies, you may find that you're overinsured in some areas and underinsured in others. You may want to call in your insurance agent to help you determine the types of insurance and the amounts that are right for you.

So, what are some of the basic types of insurance you should consider? Life insurance, disability insurance and personal liability insurance are three types of insurance that many people need, and of which we'll discuss in detail. There are also a few other types of insurance that we'll touch on briefly.

Life Insurance

What would happen to your family if you were to die today? Would your loved ones face undue financial hardship, or would they at least have the comfort of knowing their finances were in order? As difficult as it is to think about the possibility of a premature death, life insurance is one insurance need that should never be overlooked. In all likelihood, you already have life insurance. But when was the last time you reviewed or updated your policy to make sure it meets your current needs? Have you changed jobs, been promoted or bought a new or a bigger home? Has your family expanded? Or have your children grown up and moved out on their own? Any one of these lifestyle changes may signal a need to update your insurance plan. Take the time to review your life insurance needs on a regular basis and make sure that you're adequately covered so that your family will be taken care of in the event that you die.

Assuming you already have some form of life insurance, what type of policy do you have? Is it a group policy through your employer or a professional association, or is it an individual policy that you purchased on your own? Depending on your age, overall health and risk factors, either a group or an individual policy could offer you greater benefits. Premiums for group plans are calculated based on the average risk of the group; as a result, they can be helpful to higher risk individuals who would otherwise pay high premiums. On the other hand, healthy younger people with few risk factors can generally find better rates and benefits through an individual plan.

Calculating Life Insurance

Making sure you have enough life insurance is more important than the type of policy you buy. To determine how much life insurance you need, start by asking yourself the following questions:

- What expenses and debts do you have that would need to be paid upon your death (i.e., funeral expenses, probate costs, educational loans, installment debts, mortgage payments)?

- What is your current income? Calculating insurance needs solely on rough rules of thumb (i.e., six or eight times your annual income) may be inappropriate in your situation.

- What is your spouse's income? If your spouse doesn't work, would he or she do so if you were to die?

- How many children do you have? Do they plan to attend college?

• Do you have investments, savings, or other assets that survivors could draw on? If these are sizable, you may need little or no life insurance.

• Would your family receive any income from Social Security? Would that amount be reduced if your spouse was to work?

• Would your survivors need to maintain their current standard of living or could they live comfortably at a lower standard of living?

• Do you have an illiquid estate, such as real estate, that might require cash to pay estate taxes?

• What amount of tax can you or your survivors afford?

Once you've settled on your life insurance needs, you're then ready to select an appropriate life insurance policy.

Term vs. Cash Value Life Insurance

Term insurance offers "pure protection." In other words, the policy is worth its face value. Term insurance is often a good choice for young people who want a lot of protection without the expensive premiums of investment-type products. The downside to term insurance is that the premiums become increasingly expensive as you age. However, these policies can sometimes be converted to cash value policies at a later date.

Those who opt for a cash value life insurance product usually have a set premium; you pay more in your younger years than you would for a term policy, but your premiums won't increase as you age. In fact, once you've accumulated enough cash value, a loan will be drawn against the cash value to cover the premium and prevent a lapse of the policy. These policies can also be used to help finance a college education, retirement or long-term care.

Fixed vs. Variable Life Insurance

Today, many life insurance policies feature separate accounts for the investment portion, allowing policyholders to choose from a variety of bond, stock or mixed portfolio accounts. If you choose the variable option, you take an investment risk but have the opportunity to earn larger returns than offered by a fixed policy. Be advised that although variable life insurance is an insurance product it is also a security.

Disability Insurance

One asset that most individuals can't afford to lose is their income. Yet, your chances of being disabled at some point during your working years are statistically quite high. In fact, you are four times as likely to be disabled for at least 90 days during your working years than you are to die before age 65. And, if you are disabled for at least 90 days, the odds are good that your disability may last for at least five years. Despite these frightening statistics, you may have never stopped to think about what you would do if you were to become temporarily or permanently disabled or suffer from a prolonged illness. Such an event could have a devastating impact on your financial situation.

There are two types of disability insurance: short-term and long-term coverage. Short-term coverage generally lasts for 26 weeks or less; once short-term coverage expires, long-term coverage usually kicks in. As with life insurance, your employer probably offers some type of disability coverage. However, the amount offered through your workplace often is inadequate to meet your financial needs and the result would still cause financial hardship for you and your family.

Personal Liability Insurance

The primary purpose of liability insurance is to protect your assets if you're sued for damages as a result of negligence, which results in harm or injury to another person. The other reason for liability insurance is to pay defense costs. You may not think this type of insurance applies to you. However, given our current lawsuit-prone society, most people should at least consider liability insurance. Do you serve on the board of directors of a private or public company? Do you own a rental property or a swimming pool or do you have dangerous animals? For these and many other reasons, you may need some type of liability insurance. In fact, as sad as it seems, you should have some form of liability coverage even if you're just coaching your child's baseball team.

So, what types of liability insurance are available? There are three primary types of liability coverage. These include professional liability coverage, comprehensive personal liability coverage and umbrella liability coverage. In many cases, your homeowners or auto policies offer sufficient umbrella coverage. Be sure to read exclusions carefully to ascertain whether you need additional coverage.

Other Types of Insurance

Some types of insurance are designed to protect your assets, such as homeowner's or auto insurance, and are absolutely necessary. However, there are other types of insurance that are often already covered in your other insurance policies. Some such policies include credit card insurance, hospital indemnity, specific disease coverage and flight insurance.

Common Insurance Terms

Many individuals have a hard time deciphering all the terminology found in insurance documents. The following represent some of the more common terms used in the industry.

Agent: A person licensed by a state (or states) to sell insurance.

Beneficiary: The person who receives benefits or payments from an insurance policy.

Claim: A demand made by the insured, or the insured's beneficiary, for payment of benefits provided by a policy.

Coverage: The scope of protection provided under a contract.

Deductible: The amount of an insured loss paid by the policyholder. If you have a $500 deductible for auto insurance, you pay the first $500 worth of damages for your car, if you are in an accident. As deductibles increase, premiums decrease.

Exclusions: Specific situations, conditions or circumstances not covered by a policy.

Insured: The person or organization covered under an insurance policy.

Insurer: An insurance company. Also known as a carrier.

Liability: The responsibility for causing injury to someone or damage to property.

Policyholder: A person or organization that purchases insurance.

Premium: The amount of money paid or payable for coverage under an insurance policy.

Rate: The cost of a unit of insurance; the basis for the premium.

Underwriter: An insurance company employee who reviews applications for insurance to ensure they are acceptable and appropriately priced. Sometimes this term refers to an insurer.

Will You Need Long-Term Care?

Long-term care is the kind of assistance you need when you require help with personal care. The need for this assistance usually results from a disabling or long-term medical or physical condition. Long-term care services can include in-home care, as well as nursing home community care.

Who Needs Long-Term Care?

Anyone may need long-term care services. An accident or sudden serious illness can create a need for services, as can the slow progression of chronic diseases such as rheumatoid arthritis, Alzheimer's disease or Parkinson's disease. Age or fragility may also be a contributing factor. Women are more likely to need long-term care services than men since their life expectancy is about eight years longer than men. Women are twice as likely as men to enter a nursing home.

How Should You Plan for Long-Term Care?

There are a variety of home health care programs that tend to allow older people to remain independent. They rely on other people assisting those persons in need. These include personal care, homemaker services, hospice, respite care and adult day support centers. If you have to bear the brunt of this care yourself, then perhaps you should look for an assisted living facility or residential care facility. These facilities include room and board plus personal care in a supervised environment. If a higher level of care is needed, the individual may have to be cared for in a skilled nursing facility.

Is Long-Term Care Insurance Necessary?

Long-term care insurance is designed to reimburse you for some of your expenses when you need assistance with activities of daily living, such as bathing, eating or getting in and out of bed. Long-term care insurance pays for this type of care, whether it would be in institutions, like skilled nursing facilities or through assisted living facilities at home for home health care, personal care, homemaker services, hospice care and respite care and in the community for adult day care.

What Should You Know Before Purchasing a Long-Term Care Insurance Policy?

Here are a few rules of thumb to help you plan. Your policy should not exceed 7 percent of your annual income. If you have significant assets, plan to pay the premiums yourself. Premiums are based on age whereby the older you are, the more expensive the premiums will be. If you have serious health issues, it is unlikely that you would be accepted for long-term care insurance. Also, if you possess any preexisting conditions, the company may refuse to pay you during the first six months after you buy the policy. Look at the financial rating of the insurance company before purchasing. Rating companies, such as Standard & Poor's, Duff and Phelps, Moody's and A.M. Best, evaluate insurance companies on their financial condition and their claims paying ability. These ratings are available by calling up the company or from your local library.

Cost is another issue. Factors to consider include:

- Your age and your health at the time you apply for coverage.

- The deductible or waiting period you choose before the policy begins pay.

- The types of benefits you want.

- The daily benefit you want.

- The number of years you want the company to pay benefits.

Long-term care insurance is an issue you should begin planning for sooner rather than later.

LIFE INSURANCE NEEDS WORKSHEET

Use the following worksheet to estimate your life insurance needs in current dollars.

Expenses

1. Final Expenses (onetime expenses incurred by your death)

    a. Include expenses such as final illness, burial and funeral costs, Probate costs, federal estate taxes, inheritance taxes, legal fees, estate administration and other

    $\underline{\hspace{3cm}}$

2. Outstanding Debt (to be paid off at your death)

    a. Credit card/consumer debt, car, mortgage, other

    $\underline{\hspace{3cm}}$

3. Readjustment Expenses (to cover the transition period of immediate crisis)

    a. Child care, live-in nanny, vocational counseling, educational training, state inheritance taxes or other

    $\underline{\hspace{3cm}}$

4. Dependency Expenses (until all children are self-supporting)

    a. Estimate an amount for each dependent child

    $\underline{\hspace{3cm}}$

5. Education Expenses

    a. Four years' worth of private or public school tuition in current dollars $\underline{\hspace{3cm}}$

6. Life Income (for the surviving spouse after the children are all self-supporting)

    a. Annual amount desired (in current dollars) after deduction for spouse's estimated annual income multiplied by the number of years from the time the children are self-supporting and the surviving spouse qualifies for Social Security benefits $_____

7. Retirement Income for Surviving Spouse

    a. Annual amount desired in current dollars (less Social Security and any pension income) $_____

    b. Multiply by number of years of life expectancy after retirement begins:

    $_____ (Line 7a) x _____ (years) = $_____

8. Total funds needed to cover expenses: $_____

Resources

A. Proceeds from life insurance already owned $_____

B. Cash and savings $_____

C. Equity in real estate (if survivors will sell) $_____

D. Securities $_____

E. Retirement plans: your contributions $_____

F. Retirement plans: employer contributions $_____

G. Lump-sum employer pension benefits (i.e., defined benefit plans) $_____

H. Other sources $_____

9. Total assets (add lines A through H) $_____

Shortfall: Additional life insurance required

10. Subtract available assets (Line 9) from total funds needed to cover expenses (Line 8). This shortfall represents the estimated amount that must be covered through life insurance.

    $_____ (Line 8) - _____ (Line 9) = $_____

DISABILITY INCOME NEEDS WORKSHEET

The following worksheet will help you determine how much disability insurance you need.

Expenses

1. Total annual family living expenses $_____

2. Subtract annual expenses which will be eliminated should you become disabled $_____

3. Net annual family living expenses (subtract disabled expenses from annual living expenses)

$_____ (Line 1) - _____ (Line 2) = $_____

Resources

4. Annual income from savings and investments (dividends and interest) $_____

5. Annual income from spouse's job $_____

6. Disability benefits provided by employer's policy

$_____

7. Disability benefits provided by other disability policies currently owned $_____

8. Total available resources (add lines 4, 5, 6 and 7)

$_____

9. Additional resources needed either from liquidating assets or additional disability insurance (subtract Line 8 from Line 3)

$_____ (Line 3) - _____ (Line 8) = $_____

CHAPTER 7

INVESTMENT PLANNING: DEVELOPING A GAME PLAN ON HOW TO INVEST

Now that we have covered the basic financial planning needs, we are ready to invest. The key to investing right is to develop a process and follow it all the way through, while keeping a close eye on it. While results cannot be guaranteed, you can do much to reduce your exposure to risk and hopefully not sacrifice the return that you were counting on to hit your objectives that you set up in the financial planning stage.

Most successful investment portfolios will depend on the strategic decisions you make with your investments. Once that is accomplished, a tactical approach that fills in the details will be needed. We'll talk more on that later.

Uncomfortable Realities about Saving and Investing

It's easy to *not* plan ahead for savings. For many young people, their concern about funding a secure retirement does not compete with the costly and current realities of purchasing a new home and raising children. By the time they reach their 40s, thoughts of retirement start to set in—only to be pushed aside by the cost of their children's college tuition or their desire to "buy" a more opulent lifestyle. Studies show that many people wait until they pass age 50 to focus on funding their retirement. That's unfortunate because the sooner you start to save regularly and invest those savings wisely, the greater your chances of successfully meeting the financial challenges that you will face throughout your entire life.

The bottom line is this: to accomplish those objectives you set out for yourself you should save at least 10 percent of your gross income every year. Given the common financial hurdles that most of us will have to overcome in life, like the erosive effect of inflation and longer life expectancies, saving 15 to 20 percent of your income is preferable. Of course, those who prefer spending to saving will have another option: working three jobs to put their children through college, and at 75 being a Walmart greeter in order to support their own "retirement." Do you really want to be in that position?

Inflation works against your savings. When considering how much money you will need to reach your financial goals, you must factor in the impact of inflation on the cost of living. For example, assuming that inflation averages 3.5 percent per year, your living expenses will double in about 20 years. In other words, $60,000 will equal today's $30,000.

Therefore, your investment program should assure, over the long run, that your assets provide you with a return that beats inflation. Assume, for example, that inflation for a given year is 4 percent and a certificate of deposit (CD) happens to have a 4 percent return for the year. On an inflation-adjusted basis, the CD just kept pace with inflation; it produced a zero inflation-adjusted return. On top of that, if the CD interest also was subject to income taxes, it actually lost ground to inflation. On the other hand, if you have a stock mutual fund that rose by 9 percent in a year when inflation was 4 percent, this investment beat inflation handily.

One of the advantages of owning stocks and stock mutual funds is that they have generally outperformed other types of investments when held for at least five to 10 years.

Investing for a Secure Financial Future

Now that we discussed the uncomfortable elements and the importance regarding saving and investing, let's find out what you need to do in order to make investing work. There are many key ingredients to successful investing. The following five-step plan can prove beneficial to ensure your financial future.

 KNOW WHY YOU'RE INVESTING

Everyone invests for different reasons, even if we all share one overall goal: achieving ultimate financial security. Some common investment goals also might include providing an emergency fund for unforeseen events, meeting major expenses—a first home, college education, a daughter's wedding—and, most importantly, saving for a comfortable retirement. You must be clear about your investment goals in order to achieve them.

INVEST FOR GROWTH

Every investor needs to invest some money for growth to offset the effect that inflation and taxes will have.

DIVERSIFY ACROSS INVESTMENTS

Diversification is key to successful investing. No single investment category and no single industry have consistently outperformed all the others. When choosing particular areas of stocks, bonds, and mutual funds to invest in, don't bet too heavily on what's hot in the current market. Rather, consider what investment classes will continue to be attractive five and 10 years from now.

DIVERSIFY WITHIN INVESTMENTS

Diversifying among investment classes—holding a certain percentage in stocks, bonds and mutual funds—is a good start to a successful investment portfolio. Within each category of investment, however, some are going to thrive, and others will not. The best way to protect yourself from the effect of a mediocre stock, bond or mutual fund is to select more than one to invest in. You may want to hold an international stock mutual fund as well as a U.S. stock mutual fund to take advantage of investment opportunities both at home and abroad.

 5 ## TAKE CONTROL OVER YOUR INVESTMENTS

Perhaps the most important attribute of a successful investing program is to stay in touch with all your investments. Don't solely rely on someone else to watch over your portfolio and make all of your investment decisions. While professionals can make helpful suggestions, you also should be well enough informed to be able to make the final decision.

Investing is not cheap nor without risk. If it were, then everyone would be doing a great job with it and making all sorts of money. But before you can be a careful investor, you must understand the parameters that are faced when making investment decisions.

Investment Parameters

How do you define risk? The most critical component of the investment planning process is the assessment of risk. Risk involves probabilities that actual future returns will be below expected returns and may result in loss of principal. This uncertainty is created by the volatility in the marketplace.

If you understand this concept of risk, then what has happened to your investment return during the last year will make sense and your disappointment with your investment returns will have been greatly reduced. I think most individuals truly do not know their tolerance for risk. For an individual to truly know their risk tolerance, they have to ask themselves what their tolerance is for losing principal, not just returns. Essentially, how much pain can you take? Given this fact, where do your investment parameters fit in the overall investment planning process?

With a stock market on pace to having yet another lackluster finish this year, how can you tie your portfolio design to reach your investment parameters? There are six different investment parameters that help financial planners define our clients. These include risk tolerance, time horizon, liquidity, marketability, income tax consequences and diversification. These investment parameters serve as the premise in the creation of an investment policy statement. Let's discuss what they are and how they relate to constructing your portfolio.

Risk Tolerance

We've all heard the phrase that people are risk averse. That's simply not true. People are not risk averse. They are loss averse. They want great returns without any risk! The fact of the matter is that if you undertake more risk, then the propensity for reward will be that much greater.

How much risk are you willing to take? It helps if you have been around the block a few times. In other words, have you been in the market, made money and then lost that money and received the ultimate wake-up call? From what I gather, older clients tend to have less tolerance for risk simply because their time horizon is shorter. In my experience, males take on more risk than females, singles take on more than married couples and those who work for the public sector are more risk averse than those who work for the private sector. Some of you have probably used a risk tolerance questionnaire to act as an objective measure for measuring risk tolerance to help you select the right portfolio design for you. But is that really enough?

Time Horizon

Ask yourself this simple question, "When do you want the funds to fulfill this particular objective?" The answer should tie back to the data you've uncovered in the data gathering and goal formulation stage within the development of your financial plan. You need to become educated on the importance of time horizon by understanding the historical performance of the capital markets. Don't be one of those individuals who tend to underestimate their time horizons, which results in an underweighting of equities and an overexposure to inflation. Time horizon is the key variable in determining the right mix of interest-generating versus equity investments in a portfolio that tie back to long-term objectives.

As a general rule, if you have a long time horizon, you'll generally require less liquidity and can usually tolerate more risk, whereas individuals with shorter time horizons don't have the time to overcome riskier investments. For longer time horizons, the concern is one of purchasing power risk rather than volatility risk. If you have a shorter time horizon, say less than five years, don't invest in equities because you do not have the time to ride out a possible market downturn. One year or less, then its short-term accounts like money markets. Make sure you always tie back to your objectives. For example, if you have two children, ages 10 and 12, and college funding is a priority, select a time horizon between 10 and 12 years. Anything beyond 10 to 12 years would not be warranted.

Liquidity vs. Marketability

People often get these two terms confused. Liquidity means the ability to convert an asset into cash without significant loss of principal. That differs from marketability, which states whether there is a readily available marketplace to buy, sell or exchange an asset. Generally, assets are more liquid if many traders are interested in a fairly standardized product. For example, treasury bills are a highly liquid security whereas real estate and venture capital are not. Liquidity provides you with the opportunity to change your mind by correcting any errors that are made relatively easily and cheaply. Therefore, as your circumstances change, adjust your investments to stay in close harmony with your changing short-term objectives.

If you have shorter time horizons, keep more of your money in liquid types of accounts, like money market accounts, etc. For example, if you are looking to fund college relatively soon, have a fair amount of the costs in liquid accounts.

Older individuals have increased liquidity needs. For example, a 60-year-old person may need a higher reserve to fund unanticipated medical or long-term care concerns. Wealthy individuals need liquid funds to pay tax liabilities. Income tax planning will be discussed in greater detail in Chapter 10.

Marketability generally provides no liquidity. For example, your primary residence is marketable. You could sell it today if need be, but if you did, the chances of getting anything close to full potential value would be slim.

Diversification

Nowhere like the present can we see the importance of diversification. Clearly the approach of the '90s where stocks ruled does not apply today; having only stocks in your portfolio is very shortsighted. It just doesn't work like that anymore. Just as you need a properly balanced diet, you need a properly balanced portfolio, consisting of an asset allocation of stocks, bonds and cash as the core food groups. Real estate and other types of investments may be warranted as well.

Diversification gives way to asset allocation. A solid approach to asset allocation is to tie into your objectives. The two areas of focus should be capital accumulation and capital distribution. In the beginning of your investment career, you will be in the capital accumulation mode. If you have a longer time horizon, your answer as to the best way to build the nest egg is through the growth of capital. Stocks tend to be a better investment choice than other types of investments because of higher historical returns. You should have no immediate need for the funds and can therefore take on greater risks in exchange for these higher returns.

If you are in the distribution stage you should have preservation of capital and current income as your primary objectives. However, capital growth through stock allocation should not be discarded during this stage (just reduced perhaps) since the retirement period could extend as long as one-third of your lifetime. In addition, although bonds have historically produced the highest current annual income of any financial asset, bond interest income doesn't increase over time. Considering inflation, real interest income actually declines. Stock income has historically grown at the rate of inflation. Over a 10-year period, dividend income from stocks will generally exceed interest income from bonds.

Sometimes, you will need to make a trade-off between taxes and diversification needs. If you are a small business owner and have most of your wealth concentration in the equity of your small business, or if as an employee, you purchase substantial amounts of your employer's stock through payroll deduction plans during your working life, then your portfolio may contain a large amount of unrealized capital gains. In addition, the risk position of such a portfolio may be quite high, because it is concentrated in a single company. The decision to sell some of the company stock in order to diversify your portfolio's risk by reinvesting the proceeds in other assets must be balanced against the resulting tax liability.

With the volatile marketplace giving all sorts of reality checks, the inherent issues surrounding your investment parameters play an even larger role. Through this exercise, you will understand the risks and rewards pertinent to successful achievement within the investment planning process.

Asset Allocation

Asset allocation means: do not put all your eggs in one basket. Diversification is the key. Asset allocation can have many meanings and include significant issues depending on the type of investor you are.

Some of the more important issues that carry out

the diversification process include determining the tax status and after-tax implications of investments in a given asset class, your individual motivations, personal circumstances and cyclical and secular market outlook. Also pay close attention to the timing and magnitude of intergenerational income requirements, the ability to tolerate and be adequately compensated for bearing risk or loss, absolute and relative performance goals and benchmarks for measuring returns, the influence of one or more concentrated investment positions, personal holdings and collectibles and meaningful financial liabilities, such as mortgage debt.

While asset allocation can provide true benefits, some drawbacks still exist. For starters, by diversifying across major asset classes, if one asset class is a hot segment, then you will not be able to participate in potential price advances of specific asset classes.

Asset Allocation Process

There is a five-step process used for creating a disciplined asset allocation approach.

1. Examine and spell out assumptions with respect to future expected returns, risk and the correlation between asset classes.

2. Select asset classes that best match your profile and objectives that when combined provide you with the maximum expected return for a given level of risk.

3. Develop a long-term investment policy that provides you with a strategic asset allocation path.

4. Make tactical asset allocation decisions to fit into the strategic approach described above.

5. Monitor your progress and make changes when necessary.

Asset allocation is about combining the underlying characteristics of the different asset classes to provide you with the most favorable risk/return relationships. You want to set various guidelines to avoid over-relying on any one asset class when diversifying. Your objective is to increase your overall return from a portfolio for a given level of risk, or to reduce the overall risk for the portfolio for a targeted level of return. For asset allocation to achieve successful investment results over a sufficient time horizon, the right asset classes with the right properties need to be combined in the right proportions.

Allocating Investments

Investing effectively is crucial to your financial success. Therefore, you need to develop a plan that will help guide you both in deciding on the types of investments to make and in reviewing your investments periodically. Periodically doesn't mean everyday; otherwise, you'll become so concerned that you'll end up making investment changes too frequently. Rather, if you establish sensible criteria now, you will be able to invest wisely without needing to spend an inordinate amount of time worrying about your investments. The four steps to allocating your investments are:

Step 1: Decide how much of your money should be invested in stocks and how much in interest-earning securities (bonds and short-term securities).

Step 2: Once you know how much of your portfolio should be in each investment category, you will need to determine how to purchase the securities you want. You can buy individual stocks and interest-earning securities yourself, or you can take advantage of professional management by investing in mutual funds. You may very well want to use some combination of both approaches.

Step 3: For each investment category, determine what types of investments would be appropriate for your portfolio objectives and comfort level.

Step 4: Finally, you need to select and purchase the actual securities—such as a particular stock, bond or mutual fund—that will work to achieve your investment goals.

Ideally, most portfolios should contain a balanced combination of the various types of investment vehicles discussed above, interest-earning investments (both cash equivalents and bonds), stocks and, perhaps, real estate.

Once you have determined how to divide your portfolio, you can decide whether to directly—or indirectly—own your investments. Owning individual stocks or bonds is a form of direct investing, whereas buying stock or bond mutual funds is an increasingly popular form of indirect investing. Indirect investing means buying shares in a fund whose professional managers buy individual stock or bond issues for the fund investors.

Once you have allocated your assets among directly and indirectly owned investments, you need to divide these investment categories further into specific industry, market and/or fund categories. Directly owned, interest-earning investments might consist of short-term investments (money market accounts, certificates of deposit), municipal bonds, corporate bonds and Treasury bonds. If you also decide to invest in interest-earning mutual funds, you might consider a Treasury bond fund and a municipal bond fund.

Finally, you will need to select specific investments within each of the industry or mutual fund categories that you have identified. One of the most important prerequisites for investment success is asking the right questions. Familiarizing yourself with the array of commonly available investments will help you ask the right questions so that you can become a more informed investor.

The 10-Step Investment Management Action Plan Worksheet

1. Summarize all of your investments.

2. Determine how your investments are allocated, in total, among the three investment categories: stock, fixed income and cash.

3. Factor in your objectives when designing the right allocation of your investments.

4. Put "savings" first. Save on a regular basis.

5. Constantly monitor your portfolio. Don't be rash in making changes.

6. Substance over form. Make sure the investment merits outweigh everything else.

7. Taxes should be a secondary reason to invest.

8. Don't time the market; long-term buy and hold will usually work best.

9. Use mutual funds as your primary investment vehicle.

10. Don't chase returns. Keep with your long-term strategy and don't deviate from your long-term objectives.

CHAPTER 8

UNDERSTANDING INVESTMENT TYPES

Investments come in many different types. In order for you to design a portfolio based on the various asset categories, an understanding of the different types of investments is necessary.

Interest-Earning Investments

Interest-earning investments share the following characteristics: they pay interest at specified intervals, and they pay back the face value of your investment when the security matures, depending upon the type of maturity you're investing in. A bond is an interest-earning investment. However, all interest-earning investments are not bonds.

Interest-earning investments can be broken down into two categories: cash equivalents and bonds (also known as fixed-income investments).

Cash Equivalents

Cash equivalents are short-term, interest-earning securities that can be readily converted into cash with little or no change in principal value. In other words, you get your original investment back when you sell, plus you receive interest along the way. Cash-equivalent investments include money market accounts (sold by banks), money market funds (sold by mutual fund companies), savings accounts, CDs and Treasury bills. They provide stability of principal and offer interest rates that change periodically. (In contrast, bonds or fixed-income investments offer stable interest, but the principal can fluctuate.) The interest paid on cash-equivalent investments fluctuates when overall interest rates change.

Because the interest rates on cash equivalents are generally close to the inflation rate for the same period, they are best viewed as a temporary parking place for your money while you are awaiting a more attractive investment opportunity.

A bond is a certificate of debt or IOU issued by a government or corporation. It promises that the issuer, or borrower, will make payment at specified times.

Bonds are generally referred to as fixed-income investments because, in most cases, the interest rates they pay remain constant for the life of the bond. An investor who purchases a bond locks in a specific interest rate for as long as he or she owns the bond. It also means that an investor is exposed to an element of risk if interest rates should rise during this holding period.

The value of fixed-income investments moves in the opposite direction from changes in interest rates. Therefore, if interest rates rise, the value of your bond will decline, and vice versa. Some of the many available fixed-income investments include Treasury notes and bonds,

U.S. savings bonds, mortgage-backed securities, municipal bonds, corporate bonds and convertible bonds.

Treasury Securities

These securities are the means by which the U.S. government borrows money. Treasury bills, notes and bonds are issued regularly by the Federal Reserve and are a popular investment for people who want very little risk. Since these are direct obligations of the U.S. government, the interest on Treasury bills, notes and bonds is exempt from state income taxes.

Treasury bills (T-bills) are the safest investment because there is no possibility of default. Because of this safety factor, returns are not as high as other types of investments. Generally, T-bills keep pace with inflation in the long run.

Treasury notes have time horizons of one to 10 years and offer near-absolute protection from default on principal and interest. They do, however, pose one significant investment risk, which is of rising interest rates. A note or bond yielding a fixed coupon will decline in market value when interest rates rise, and the longer the maturity of the note, the greater the damage. At a maturity of five years, the loss in principal market value can exceed the coupon of the note or bond, resulting in negative total return for the year. For bearing this risk, you are rewarded additional long-term return.

Treasury bonds have time horizons greater than 10 years up to 30 years. You would expect these returns to be the best of this bunch because of the longer time horizon. But actually, you are not rewarded at all for bearing this risk. The return is almost identical to that of a five-year Treasury note.

Bonds

Bonds represent lending money to companies. Technically, it is legal evidence of a debt, usually the result of lending money to a company. When you buy a bond, you are lending your money to the issuer of the bond. The issuer agrees to make periodic payments to you, the investor holding the bond and also agrees to pay the principal in full by the maturity date of the bond. You will be paid the full amount at maturity regardless of where interest rates head during your ownership of the bond. Interest payments are certain and there will be no volatility with the investment.

The key to investing in bonds is to know what backs the bond. For example, corporate bonds are backed by the company's full faith and credit concerning its ability to pay the bond. These bonds are also called debenture bonds.

There are many different bond types that can be broken down into three categories: U.S. obligations, municipal obligations and corporate obligations.

United States (U.S.) Obligations

U.S. Savings Bonds

These are a popular way for savers to invest in government securities. Although they don't offer the highest rate of interest, savings bonds are a sound and comfortable way for investors to build up their savings.

Mortgage-Backed Securities

These securities have peculiar-sounding names like Ginnie Mae, Fannie Mae and Freddie Mac. These investments represent pools of mortgages backed by the specific government agency. They can be bought either individually or through mutual funds, which offer a wider degree of diversification and security.

Municipal Obligations

Municipal Bonds

Municipal bonds are used to finance long-term projects for cities, towns, villages, territories and states. They are very popular investments because the interest they generate is free from federal taxation. Sometimes, if you purchase bonds of issuing authorities in your own state (or bonds of Puerto Rico and other U.S. territories), the interest is also exempt from state income taxes and, perhaps, local income taxes. These investments also can be purchased individually, or through a family of mutual funds.

Corporate Obligations

Corporate Bonds

Corporations issue bonds to raise money just like the

U.S. government and state governments. Due to changing economic conditions, some corporate bonds are no longer the safe haven for investors' money that they used to be. Too much borrowing and the sometimes rapidly deteriorating financial condition of corporations require careful selection and monitoring. Therefore, investors of corporate bonds are well-advised to stick with highly rated bonds.

Convertible Bonds

These are corporate bonds that can be converted into stock at a predetermined price. They are more attractive to some investors than, say, regular bonds because they enable investors to gain from the appreciation of the underlying common stock. However, this conversion privilege usually means their yields are one or more percentage points below those of a straight bond.

Four Investment Risks You Need to Know About

Some people mistakenly think of bonds as staid, riskless investments. But like stock investing, bond investing isn't risk free. Four risks you should know about that affect the bond market are:

1. **Interest Rate Risk.** This is the risk that your investment's value will fluctuate with changes in the general level of interest rates. Because interest rates can fluctuate widely over the course of a year, price vola-

tility is a factor that must be considered in planning and selecting fixed-income investments. Of course, when it comes to investing in a bond fund, such planning is left to experienced managers who are in touch with the day-to-day changes in the bond market and the overall economy.

In general, if interest rates rise, the market value of a bond declines. Conversely, if interest rates decline, the market value of a bond increases.

2. **Purchasing Power Risk.** This is the risk that a bond will lose purchasing power if inflation heats up. Because bonds have set interest rates and pay back the principal at a future date, they do not offer an inflation hedge.

3. **Credit Risk.** This is the risk of default by the bond issuer. In other words, it's the risk that you won't get your money back or the issuer won't make an interest payment. This is why corporate and municipal bonds are risk rated by rating agencies such as Standard & Poor's Corporation and Moody's Investors Service, Inc.

4. **Call Risk.** This is the risk that a bond will be called, or bought back prior to maturity by the issuer on demand. This generally takes place after interest rates have declined substantially. Calling a bond then allows the issuer to reissue the bonds at a much lower

interest rate. Investors in bonds that are called will then have to reinvest their money at lower interest rates.

Interest-Earning Investment Strategies

The best time to purchase bonds (or bond mutual funds) is when you think interest rates are high and are unlikely to rise further and/or are likely to fall.

Fluctuating interest rates combined with the proliferation of many different kinds of bonds have discouraged many people from investing in these types of instruments. Instead, they are content with short-term securities such as money market funds. Yet, with a little effort, they might be able to increase investment returns by taking advantage of the many bond investments that are available today.

The following nine tips will help you make savvy bond investments.

Tips for Investing in Bonds

 1 SEEK EXPERTISE WHEN NECESSARY

Investments in bonds that you are unfamiliar with, such as foreign bonds, should definitely be made through a mutual fund with management specializing in these areas.

KEEP AN EYE ON PRICE VOLATILITY

Since interest rate can fluctuate widely over the course of a year, price volatility is a factor that must be taken into account in planning and selecting bonds. Generally speaking, the longer the maturity date, the more volatile the price of that particular issue.

 LADDER MATURITIES

Laddering, or staggering the maturities of bond investments, is a tried and true strategy. Rather than investing in a single issue or in several issues with roughly the same maturity, you should opt for a variety of maturities—some short term (less than three years), some intermediate term (three to 10 years) and some long term (10 to 30 years). That way, if there is a significant change in interest rates, you will have avoided placing a heavy, and perhaps incorrect, bet on a single maturity. Simply stated, laddering maturities reduces the risk in any bond portfolio. Don't forget to set some of the maturities to coincide with when you may need the money (for instance, to meet college tuition bills or to provide money during your retirement years). If you invest in bond mutual funds, you also can follow a similar laddering strategy by spreading your money among money market and short-term bond funds, intermediate-term bond funds and long-term bond funds.

④ COMPARE INTEREST RATES

Interest rates vary among different types of bonds, both within the same investment category and between alternative categories. For example, if you shopped around a little, you might discover that the rate paid on CDs at your local bank is not as good as it might be. Over the past several years, interest rates on tax-exempt bonds have been very attractive compared with the after-tax returns on Treasury securities and corporate bonds.

⑤ DON'T CHASE YIELD

While shopping for yield is a virtue, chasing yield is a sin. A bond investment that pays 10 percent interest when other bonds of the same type and maturities are at 6 percent is trying to tell you something. This probably is a junk bond (high-yielding, highly risky type of bond that has a low, speculative credit rating) or similarly risky investment. Don't be fooled. Always remember, the higher the yield, the higher the risk.

⑥ DIVERSIFY

It is never wise to concentrate your interest-earning

investments in a single or very few securities. Select several different issues and several different categories of investments or mutual funds.

 7 KEEP MATURITIES RELATIVELY SHORT

Even though long-maturity, interest-earning investments usually have higher yields than short-maturity investments, many experts contend that there is usually not enough of a difference to justify the greater risks in concentrating on long-maturity bonds. Remember, the longer the maturity, the more the value of the bond will fluctuate in reaction to changes in interest rates.

 8 USE MUTUAL FUNDS FOR INVESTING IN UNUSUAL BONDS

If you want to invest in foreign bonds, chances are you won't have the time or ability to track the market as closely as a smart investor needs to do. By investing in a foreign bond mutual fund, you can diversify the bond portion of your portfolio and, at the same time, take advantage of the professional manager's foreign bond expertise.

9 CONSIDER THE TAX EFFECTS

You may be able to increase your investment returns by carefully examining the tax effects of alternative interest-earning investments. While some are fully taxable, interest on Treasury securities is federally taxable but exempt from state taxes. Municipal bond interest is exempt from federal taxes and may be exempt from state taxes. It is important to keep in mind that the federally taxable securities should be purchased for your tax-deferred retirement accounts. Tax-favored investments like municipal bonds should be purchased for your personal investment account.

Purchasing Interest-Earning Investments

You can buy cash-equivalent or bond investments directly by buying individual securities through banks or financial advisors, or indirectly through a mutual fund where, in essence, you buy a portion of a diversified portfolio of interest-earning securities. You need to evaluate how interest-earning investments fit into your overall investment portfolio (including your retirement accounts) and then decide the kinds of interest-earning securities that are most suitable. While interest-earning investments belong in every portfolio, the proportion of these investments in your total portfolio, as well as the type of investment vehicles will depend on your particular financial situation and objectives.

Stocks

This section is designed to help you make an informed decision about stock investing. It will explore such areas as what stocks are, their advantages and risks, how you can tell if they're the right investment for you and how you can select and purchase them.

Why is investing in stocks so important? If you are not investing in today's stock market, you risk falling short of realizing your financial goals. Why? Stocks have consistently proven to be the best inflation-beating vehicle for long-term investors. And if your investments aren't beating inflation, you're losing ground to the ever-increasing costs of living.

What are the Risks?

There are risks to stock investing. For example, along with the opportunity of increasing stock prices, investors also must accept the risk that stock prices will decline.

How Stocks are Classified

There are a wide variety of common stock investments. Some pay dividends; others don't. Some have relatively stable prices; others are more volatile. Despite this variety, most common stocks can be classified into one of the following categories.

Growth Stocks

Investors buy growth stocks for capital appreciation. Because many companies have to finance their growth and may be involved in expensive research, most or all of their earnings are reinvested in the company for future expansion. Thus, growth stocks have the potential for increased market value, but they pay little in dividends. Therefore, prices of growth stocks are usually more volatile than those of other stocks.

Income Stocks

Income stocks are bought for current income because they tend to have a higher-than-average dividend yield. Companies whose stocks fall into this category are usually in fairly stable industries (for example, telecommunications and utilities), have strong finances and pay out a substantial portion of their earnings in dividends. Many of the stocks are considered total return stocks because they offer the opportunity for both dividends and capital appreciation.

Blue-Chip Stocks

Blue-chip stocks are considered the highest quality of all common stocks because they are dominant companies that have the ability to pay steady dividends in both good and bad times. For example, all of the 30 stocks that compose the Dow Jones Industrial Average are blue-chip stocks.

Cyclical Stocks

Cyclical stocks are those represented by companies

whose earnings tend to fluctuate sharply with their business's cycles. When business conditions are good, a cyclical company's profitability is high and the price of its common stock rises. When conditions deteriorate, the company's sales, profits and market price fall sharply. For example, when interest rates are high and business conditions slow down, the housing and steel industries suffer tremendously. The timing of ownership is crucial to a successful investment in cyclical stocks.

Defensive Stocks

In contrast to cyclical stocks, some companies are considered recession resistant. They sell products or provide services whose demand does not fluctuate with business cycles. Examples include food, cosmetics and health care stocks.

Small Company Stocks

Small company stocks, also known as small cap stocks, are stocks of companies that typically have a total stock market value of less than $500 million. These stocks are usually traded on the over-the-counter market. Historically, small company stocks have outperformed larger company stocks—but they are more volatile because smaller companies usually have less stable and predictable earnings, and/or they may have insufficient assets to weather a business downturn.

Speculative Stocks

In a sense, all common stocks are speculative, since they

offer a variable rather than a fixed return like a bond. But some stocks are more speculative than others. A speculative stock is subject to wider swings in share price—down as well as up—so it's riskier. For example, hot new issues, high-flying glamour stocks and penny stocks are speculative stocks.

Recommendations for Investing in Stocks

There are no guarantees for stock investment success, but there are many ideas that may prove to be helpful to you. Here are 10 of them.

 NEVER BUY STOCKS INDISCRIMINATELY

Many investors buy stocks haphazardly simply because they have money to invest. This is a very bad practice; make investments only when you have a good reason to buy them.

 SELECT A PROMISING INDUSTRY

At any given time, most industries in the economy are either on the upswing or the downswing. When choosing a stock, start by selecting a promising industry with a good future outlook. Then, look for a company within that industry whose prospects look the most promising.

3 DIVERSIFY

Try to own stocks in several different industries. The danger of too many eggs in one basket can't be overemphasized.

 4 BUY LOW AND SELL HIGH

You don't necessarily have to be a contrarian to condition yourself to buy stock when a company's share price is down and sell it when the price is up. Stocks can gain when prices are low, and major selling opportunities come when the stock is hot (everybody wants to own it) and prices are high. This is the famous buy low, sell high rule; it's recommended that you use caution when following this or any other stock market strategy.

 5 STAY ABREAST OF MARKET TRENDS

Look at the general trend in the market. A stock that already has risen in value might be a good candidate for continued gains if the market is still rising. Conversely, a stock that does not respond to a general market rise might turn out to be a candidate for selling.

6 USE STOP-LOSS ORDERS TO PROTECT AGAINST LOSS

Potential losses can be effectively limited by using stop-loss orders (they're not available on over-the-counter stocks), which fence in gains by restricting the effects of a market downturn on your stocks. Stop-loss orders also can be used against you to force you to sell. For example, say you buy a stock at $12 per share and it rises to $18 per share. You might put a stop-loss order in at $15 per share to lock in a gain. The risk of this strategy is that you might get left behind at $15 per share if the stock continues rising, but this may be less risky than a loss due to a sharp decline.

7 BUY VALUE

Companies with strong finances (little debt) and solid earnings growth are consistently better long-run performers.

8 BUY LOW P/E HIGH-DIVIDEND STOCKS

Many successful long-term investors use the investment strategy of purchasing common stocks of companies with relatively low price to earnings multiples and relatively high-dividend yields. The logic behind this is that the stock price is depressed (a low P/E multiple), and hence, the stock is being purchased when no one else wants it. This is in itself a good strategy as long as the company has no major long-term problems. Moreover, when the stock price rises, the company probably will attempt to maintain its high-dividend yield by raising its dividend. Investors, therefore, get the best of both worlds: rising stock price and higher dividend income.

 BUY STOCKS IN COMPANIES WITH STRONG DIVIDEND RECORDS

Consider stocks in companies that have a consistent history of paying generous dividends. In a bear market (in which stock prices have declined), these companies tend to decline less in price than companies that pay no dividend at all or pay dividends erratically, since investors are confident that the dividends will keep coming through thick and thin. Some companies have paid annual dividends for more than 100 years.

 RELY ON YOUR OWN EXPERIENCE AND JUDGMENT

Often, looking for successful companies to invest in doesn't require that you go to Wall Street. Investment ideas can come from your own observations of how things are selling on Main Street. This common-sense strategy (on Wall

Street, it's known as real economics) has been used by some of the most successful investors and money managers for years. The next time you go to the mall, keep your eyes open for new investment opportunities.

Investment Schedule

Summarize all of your investment holdings.

DESCRIPTION	# Shares or Face Value	Date Acquired	Original Cost	Current Market Value	Estimated Annual Interest or Dividend
1. CASH & CASH EQUIVALENTS					
Savings Accounts					
CDs					
Money Market Accounts					
Other					
TOTAL CASH-EQUIVALENT INVESTMENTS					
2. FIXED-INCOME INVESTMENTS					
U.S. Obligations					
Municipal Obligations					
Corporate Bonds					

DESCRIPTION	# Shares or Face Value	Date Acquired	Original Cost	Current Market Value	Estimated Annual Interest or Dividend
Bond Funds					
GNMAs/FNMAs					
Other Fixed-Income Investments					
TOTAL FIXED-INCOME INVESTMENTS					
3. EQUITY					
Stocks					
Stock Mutual Funds					
Other Equity Investments					
TOTAL EQUITY INVESTMENTS					
4. REAL ESTATE					
Direct Ownership					
Indirect Ownership/REITs					
5. OTHER INVESTMENTS					
GRAND TOTAL INVESTMENTS					

CHAPTER 9

THE BASICS OF MUTUAL FUNDS

A mutual fund is a professionally managed investment company that pools investors' money and uses it to purchase a diversified portfolio of stocks, bonds, money market instruments or other securities. Each share in a mutual fund represents a small slice of the mutual fund's total portfolio.

What are other benefits associated with investing in mutual funds? Owning mutual funds is a low-cost way to diversify your investments, thereby reducing investment risk. Also, mutual funds are managed by experienced professionals who are responsible for monitoring and managing the stocks and/or bond holdings continuously. There are other benefits as well. You can add to your fund investments regularly and easily. Bookkeeping tasks, such as depositing dividend and interest checks and keeping track of securities transactions, are avoided. You have access to a number of convenient services, such as an option to automatically reinvest dividends, capital gains and automatic investments at regular intervals and you can easily keep up-to-date on the performance of the funds you invest in since they're listed in the financial pages of the newspaper. They are liquid, essentially allowing you to purchase or sell at will.

Of course, there are drawbacks. For one thing, like the securities they invest in, a stock or bond fund's asset value will fluctuate with changing market conditions. For another, the commission and fee structures of mutual funds can be confusing. The funds range from no-loads, which carry no sales commission and are sold directly to the public, to load funds, which typically charge commissions of 1 percent to 8.5 percent. Some funds assess a charge if you redeem your fund shares within a specified period of time. Some funds also charge a sales distribution fee each year you hold the fund.

Mutual fund investors can't control the timing of capital gains taxes since it is the fund manager who makes the decisions about selling fund holdings. In contrast, if you held individual stocks or bonds, you could control the timing of capital gains recognition by simply selling or deferring the sale of a particular stock.

Mutual Fund Categories

Mutual funds vary in size, objective and the type of investments they hold. As a result, knowing how and why they differ is important. First, there are three major fund categories:

1. **Stock funds.** A stock (or equity) mutual fund invests its money in stocks of individual companies, large and small, new and old, here and abroad.

2. **Bond funds.** A bond mutual fund invests its money in bonds of companies or governments that are as varied as those that stock funds invest in.

3. **Money market funds.** A money market fund invests its money in short-term financial instruments such as Treasury bills and CDs.

Second, there are many different types of stock and bond funds, characterized both by the kind of securities the fund invests in, and by the fund's particular objective. The following list explains the most common types of stock and bond mutual funds.

Stock Funds

Maximum Capital Gains Funds. Also called aggressive growth funds, these attempt to achieve very high returns by investing in more speculative stocks, maximizing capital gains while generating little or no income from dividends. The potential for greater rewards is linked with increased volatility and greater risk in these funds.

Small Company Growth Funds. Also called emerging growth funds, these are a type of maximum capital gain fund specializing in stocks of promising small, emerging growth companies.

Long-Term Growth Funds. These seek capital gains from companies that have the potential for steady growth in earnings. Less volatile, and more consistent than maximum capital gains funds, growth funds aim to achieve a rate of growth that beats inflation.

Growth and Income Funds. These funds seek a more balanced stock portfolio that will achieve capital appreciation as well as current income from dividends. They are less risky than growth funds, because the dividend may offset at least some of the periodic losses in stock prices.

Equity-Income Funds. These generally invest most of their portfolio in dividend-paying stocks and the rest in convertible securities and bonds. Income funds may have capital growth as a secondary objective to providing current income.

International Stock Funds. These funds provide additional diversification to a portfolio. Most international funds invest throughout the world. Some invest only in one country or region. Global stock funds, however, differ only in that they also invest in U.S. securities.

Bond Funds

Within each bond fund category, there are usually several funds that specialize in investments of either short-term, intermediate-term or long-term duration. Bond funds pay monthly income. Except for funds that invest solely in government bonds, all bond funds have some degree of risk of default. However, the real risk of bond funds is that high inflation will outpace the returns and/or rising interest rates will reduce the principal value of the investment.

Corporate Bond Funds. These buy and trade bonds of corporations. There are two categories of corporate bond mutual funds: investment-grade corporate bond funds, which comprise high-quality corporate bonds and seek high income with limited credit risk and high-yield (junk bond) bond funds, which offer potentially greater rewards with higher risk.

Government Bond Funds. Government bond funds own securities that are backed by the full faith and credit of the U.S. government. These funds offer total protection from bond default, although the value of government bonds will fluctuate with interest rates like all bonds and bond funds. One variety of government bond funds, government mortgage funds, holds mortgage-backed securities such as those issued by the Government National Mortgage Association (GNMA). Holders of mortgage funds receive both interest and a partial return of principal which may be reinvested.

Municipal Bond Funds. These provide investors with a means for tax-free income. Interest earned from bonds not issued in the investor's own state is fully taxable in his or her own state, so in order to produce maximum tax-free income, single-state funds have been developed. For example, a New York resident investor owning the New York Muni Fund will avoid state as well as federal taxes on the fund's interest income.

Convertible Bond Funds. These funds are bonds or preferred stock that can be exchanged for a fixed number of shares in the common stock of the issuing company. Convertible bond funds combine features of both stocks and bonds.

International Bond Funds. These typically invest primarily in high-quality foreign government or corporate bonds.

Specialized Stock and Bond Funds

Specialized funds offer mutual fund investors even more choices. However, the more specialized a fund becomes, the more risk it presents to the investor.

Balanced Funds. These funds maintain a balanced combination of common stocks, bonds and perhaps preferred stocks. Balanced funds offer both income and growth because they hold both bonds and stocks. One of the advantages of balanced funds is the forced discipline that they impose on the fund manager. As stock prices rise, the fund manager is forced to sell stocks to bring the portfolio back into balance. Conversely, if stock prices decline, the fund manager will purchase more stock to bring the fund back to balance.

Specialized Industry Funds. Also known as sector funds, they invest only in the stocks of a single industry, such as biotechnology, waste management, utilities, health services or energy. Sector funds, unlike traditional mutual funds, zero in on a particular area of the stock market. With sector funds, you lose the advantage of an already diversified portfolio because the fund concentrates in one industry.

Asset Allocation Funds. These invest in stock, bond, money market, real estate markets and more so that any one market's loss may be offset by another's gain. In general, asset allocation funds are supposed to represent a one-stop fund for investors who want all the advantages of diversification in one account.

Precious Metal Funds. Often called gold funds, precious metal funds usually invest in stocks of gold-mining firms and other companies engaged in the business of precious metals. Some funds may actually purchase and store the metal itself.

Index Funds and Exchange Traded Funds (ETFs). These funds replicate the performance of all of the stocks in an index, for example, the Standard & Poor's 500. They simply duplicate a broad section of the market and are attractive to investors who want their investments to do the same. Usually the expenses of such a fund are very low in comparison with those of other stock funds. In the case of an ETF, investors are able to trade the fund like a stock at any point during market hours. In essence, it is a fund that trades like a stock.

Socially Responsible Funds. These limit their investments to companies considered to be socially responsible. For example, some of these funds do not invest in companies that manufacture defense-related or tobacco products.

Money Market Funds. These constitute the most widely held mutual fund category. Three main objectives of money market funds are preservation of capital, liquidity and earning as high an income as can be achieved without sacrificing the first two objectives. Money market funds offer excellent liquidity; an investor need only write a check to transfer money. They provide liquidity because of the types of instruments they invest in, for example, Treasury bills and CDs. These funds are commonly used as a place to hold funds temporarily until new stock or bond investment opportunities arise. U.S. government money market funds and tax-exempt money market funds invest in short-term instruments of the U.S. government and states/municipalities, respectively. As with municipal bond funds, there are also some single-state tax-exempt money market funds.

CHAPTER 10

INCOME TAX PLANNING: PRESERVING YOUR ASSETS

It has been said that the only things you can count on in life are death and taxes. Even if this is true, few people enjoy thinking about either one. But income tax planning is much more than simply filling out the necessary tax forms once a year. A comprehensive financial plan that includes income tax planning can help minimize Uncle Sam's piece of the pie, and leave you with a bigger piece. Even if you only file a simple return, appropriate tax planning can help you keep more of what you earn. However, to have the biggest impact on your taxes, you need to plan year-round—not just in the weeks leading up to April 15th.

Studies show that 92 percent of Americans fail to take advantage of substantial tax deductions. The reason for this may be blamed in part on the complexity of tax laws. To further complicate the situation, these laws change every year. Most people find it difficult to keep up with these changes. As a result, you miss out on many tax-saving opportunities that could potentially save you thousands of dollars.

Does Income Tax Planning Relate to Financial Planning?

Absolutely! In fact, income tax planning is one of the essential ingredients necessary when constructing a financial plan. You always need to be concerned about the tax elements of investing for your own account or even through your retirement plan. But you should never make any financial decisions solely based on the income tax effect. By looking at your individual tax return, you may notice several areas that need immediate financial attention.

Getting Ready to File

There are several ways that you can prepare to file your tax return. You should maintain complete and well-organized records throughout the year. Your tax record keeping should be coordinated with your personal record-keeping system to ensure that all your expenses are being tracked and that all income is reported. The IRS has many publications that provide the background you need to help you in preparing your return. In particular, Publication 17 provides information on all income and deductible aspects of your personal tax return. You should make sure that good records are kept for your expenses since some of them may be deductible.

Taxation of Investments

Investments are taxed when they are sold. The tax consequences result in either capital gain income or loss, or ordinary income or loss. If you hold a security for more than a 12-month period, you incur capital gains or losses on the transaction. If it's less than 12 months, you incur ordinary income loss on the transaction. Gains result from receiving more than your purchase price, while losses result from receiving less. Through proper tax planning, if you incur gains or losses for the year, you may then wish to offset them by realizing capital gains or losses on other investments. Remember that you can deduct capital losses against other income up to $3,000 per year.

Not all investments are taxed. In fact, many investors can benefit from investing in municipal securities, especially if you are in a high marginal tax bracket. Your marginal tax bracket represents the tax rate on the last dollar of income you earned. With few exceptions, interest earned on municipal investments is exempt from federal income taxes, and if the investments are related to the state you reside in, can be free of state income tax as well.

Some Simple Long-Term Tax Planning Strategies

Tax planning consists of much more than simply taking advantage of every possible deduction. In fact, there are many tax strategies that are simple to use, as long as you meet the criteria. One strategy is if you have the opportunity to contribute to a 401(k) plan, you should. Any contribution by you reduces your taxable income by the same amount. If your company matches part or all of your contribution, then your total return will be better than most other investments you could make. If you are not part of a retirement plan offering a 401(k) plan, then you should contribute to an individual retirement account.

Another strategy is to take advantage of any deductions that apply to your situation. Certain deductions can be taken only if your total is greater than a certain amount. For example, medical expenses are deductible to the extent that you exceed 7.5 percent of adjusted gross income. Miscellaneous deductions, such as tax return preparation fees, the cost of a safety deposit box, professional dues or unreimbursed employee expenses, are deductible only to the extent you exceed 2 percent of adjusted gross income. The problem is that these thresholds are often difficult to reach in a single year. However, by bunching expenses every other year, you might exceed these minimums and make full use of these deductions. Filing separate tax returns may also get you there. Of course, this type of strategy requires advance planning.

Charitable donations of stock whose value has increased is another good strategy. Here you can take a deduction for the fair market value of the stock thus avoiding any capital gains tax. Non-cash charitable donations, such as clothing, books, computers and even furniture are also deductible at fair market value.

You can supplement your retirement income if you

have any self-employment income from a full-time or part-time business. You may be able to make a deductible contribution to a Keogh or simplified employee pension account and reduce your current taxable income.

If you're on the edge of a tax bracket, a change in income or itemized deductions could affect your tax rate. If you expect your tax rate to remain the same or to decline in the future, you may want to defer income while accelerating itemized deductions such as state withholding tax. If your tax liability increases because your income increases, make sure that you pay at least 90 percent of your current tax bill before the year's end in order to avoid any penalties.

There are many other deductions that can be written off on your tax return. For example, the government encourages home ownership. As a result, mortgage interest and real property taxes are deductible. Also points paid to secure a mortgage are also deductible. Other types of taxes, such as state tax withheld or personal property tax, are also deductible.

Job-related expenses and moving expenses are also deductible. If you move to a new work location that is 50 miles further than your old home, you may deduct the cost of the move. If you incur expenses job hunting, or even on the job, such as travel, entertainment, education expenses, work-related clothes that are not suitable for ordinary attire, business gifts or even an automobile expense, you may write this off as well.

There are many other types of deductions. Some of

these may include penalty on early withdrawal of savings, self-employment tax, union or professional dues, casualty losses, worthless securities, personal property taxes, state and local income tax, medical expenses (in excess of 7.5 percent of adjusted gross income, AGI), out-of-pocket expenses for charitable activities, gambling losses to the extent of gambling winnings and tax return preparation fees.

Effective income tax planning is both a year-round process and a multi-year process. It is much more than simply taking advantage of every possible deduction. Rather, it consists of developing a coherent, long-term strategy to reduce taxes over the years. By doing a little homework, you can become tax savvy. Proper record keeping and planning will start you on your way and help ensure that you minimize your tax burden.

Year-End Tax Issues

Many individuals don't do much to improve their tax situation. They respond after the fact, being reactive, instead of planning before the fact and being proactive. There are things you can do to help yourself in this area.

It is important to plan for year-end taxes during the fourth quarter. That's because you might be able to reduce your tax liability for the year. After January 1st, it will be too late to do anything about it and you will be stuck with your unadjusted tax liability. The following areas are things you may be able to do to improve your tax situation.

① EXPENSE NOW

For the small business owner, probably the most critical issue is the improved use of the IRC Section 179 deduction. The Sec. 179 election has been increased to $250,000 for qualified business expenses purchased during the current year. It may be phased out with too high an income level. That means that if you placed $250,000 of assets in service during the current year, you can immediately write-off up to $250,000 of taxable income from all trades or businesses. Examples of qualifying assets include all types of office equipment, off-the-shelf computer software and even a light truck or truck weighing at least 6,000 pounds (again, used for business).

② MAX OUT RETIREMENT CONTRIBUTIONS

Maximize retirement contributions. For the small business owner, establish a simplified employee pension (SEP) plan. Contributions can result from your primary business or even a side business where the employee client is covered under a Section 401(k) plan. Under a SEP arrangement, self-employed persons may contribute up to the lesser of 25 percent of the net earnings from the trade or business or $49,000. For the employee, max out the $16,000 ($21,000 if over age 50) into a 401(k) plan.

3 IRAs

Even if you are covered under a qualified plan, you can still contribute up to the IRA maximum (double if married) to an IRA. If your income is less than IRS thresholds, you may still make a deductible IRA contribution. If you earn greater than those amounts, then a Roth IRA would suffice, since the phase out limits are significantly higher.

4 INVESTMENT ISSUES

Sell off individual stocks or bonds to offset capital gains and losses generated from mutual fund redemptions. That's because mutual funds typically generate capital gains through December distributions, and this gives you the opportunity to possibly offset some of those gains. Remember, excess losses (those amounts over ordinary income) can be deducted up to $3,000 for individuals who are married filing jointly, and $1,500 for individuals who are married filing separately. Using individual security sales could therefore help minimize the tax implications.

Also, if you are thinking about selling mutual funds, when determining capital gain or loss, make sure you add all reinvested dividends, interest, capital gain distributions and sales charges to the original cost basis. By including these previously taxed items, your taxable income will be reduced, or the deductible loss will be even greater.

If you want to dispose of certain securities for tax purposes but like the long-term prognosis of the stock, in order to avoid the 30-day wash sale rules, you can sell it now and repurchase the security before year-end. If you sell the stock on November 1st, you can buy it back anytime after December 1st and before year-end to recognize the tax loss.

Again, never do things solely for tax purposes. Rather, make sure the investments are no longer economically viable. You can do this by looking at your investment portfolio.

Delay tax on interest income by transferring these accounts to certificates that mature beyond the two months remaining this year. When the certificates mature is when the interest income is recognized. Convert taxable income into commercial annuities or tax-exempt municipal bonds that grow tax-deferred. This will reduce 1099 amounts reported to the government.

When you trade business or investment property for "like kind" property, this defers recognition of gain or loss. The gain only temporarily escapes taxation, but can defer it for many years.

Before selling rental real estate, occupy your vacation home for two years in order to make it your principal residence and permanently exempt up to $500,000 of capital gain if filing married jointly, or up to $250,000 if filing single.

Also, consider Section 529 contributions. Although this won't let you reduce federal taxes, it will help you with state tax deductions or credits on those contributions.

 ## REDUCE ESTIMATE TAX PAYMENTS

If your income stayed the same or went down from last year, less estimated tax payments would be due for the current year. You can figure out how much you need to pay directly by accessing the IRS's website (www.irs.gov) and entering "Estimated Tax Payments (Individuals)" into the search field and then clicking on the appropriate link. To avoid underpayment penalties, make sure you withhold 100 percent of last year's income tax liability or 110 percent if adjusted gross income for the current year is more than $150,000.

 ## DELAY TACTIC

Reduce revenue by postponing your billings until after January 1st in order to delay collections of revenue. As self-employed business owners, you have complete control in invoicing yourself. Delaying client billings into the next year enables you to report less income and pay less tax this year. Or, if bonuses or other types of commissions need to be paid, delay those payments as well.

If you have educational funding issues, delaying billings could also help when filing financial aid applications or when cashing out of U.S. savings bonds for educational purposes, since these benefits are derived from having adjusted gross income under various thresholds. The flip side of delaying revenue is that if the economy does not get better, and deficits continue to mount, a tax increase is always a possibility. In that case, you would be deferring revenues until a year in which more tax needs to be paid on that revenue. You can also think about deferring compensation immediately. These agreements must be negotiated in advance.

⑦ ALL IN THE FAMILY

If possible, employ your children in the family business. Of course, the jobs need to be commensurate with your experience level, but can prove valuable toward the funding of a child's IRA. From an employer standpoint, if you run an incorporated business, such as an S corporation or limited liability company, wages would be paid to the children and employment taxes must be paid on your behalf. However, if you run an unincorporated business as a Schedule C taxpayer, employment taxes do not have to be taken out. Either way, the business owner's net income will be reduced by the amount of wages paid. From the child's standpoint, if the child decides to open a traditional IRA, then taxable income is reduced by the amount of IRA contribution. If a Roth is used instead, then tax is paid on the income (usually at the child's marginal tax rate which is probably the lowest level) and monies can come out of the Roth income tax-free.

Income splitting allows you to divide income among several persons or taxpaying entities that will enable you to pay an aggregate tax lower than the tax you would pay yourselves. Creating family-limited partnerships, transferring unearned income to children (just be aware of any kiddie tax implications), establishing custodial accounts and designing certain types of trust relationships are just a few examples.

If you are taking care of a dependent relative and furnish more than 50 percent of that person's financial support, you can take the dependency exemption for that person. Furthermore, if you pay for dependent medical expenses, then those expenses are deductible in addition to your own.

8 GIVE!

Accelerate charitable contributions. You can do this by making gifts of appreciated stock. You will get a tax deduction for the fair market value of the stock and not have to pay capital gains tax on its sale, thus reducing gross income. If the stock to be gifted is a loser, sell the stock first and claim the capital loss, and then donate the proceeds to the charity.

9 DON'T DELAY WHAT YOU CAN DO TODAY

Incorporate traditional acceleration strategies including prepaying state and local income taxes and the mortgage payment, purchasing low-dollar supplies for the following year and renewing subscriptions and obligations before year-end.

Whenever there is a deduction floor for expenses, there is an opportunity for bunching. Bunching expenses means that you may not have sufficient expenses to deduct those amounts annually. Having expenses that fall short of the floor doesn't provide any current tax benefit. However, bunching enables you to recognize these expenses every other year, thus receiving a deduction every second year. Examples would include miscellaneous and medical expenses.

Bunching enables you to maximize deductions every other year, so you don't have to satisfy the underlying thresholds of 2 percent for miscellaneous and 7.5 percent for medical annually. Pick the year in which your AGI will be lower. The exception to this rule is if you are a candidate for alternative minimum tax (AMT). If this is the case, you will lose your value in the regular tax year. That's because Schedule A deductions for state and local income taxes, real property taxes, miscellaneous itemized deductions and personal exemptions are all disallowed for AMT purposes. These deductions must be added back to taxable income to arrive at AMT income.

In addition, interest paid on home equity debt may not be deductible for AMT purposes even though such interest paid on up to $100,000 of debt can be claimed to arrive at the regular tax.

If you loaned money to someone, and are now unable to collect the amount owed, you can claim a deduction for this bad debt. This "non-business" bad debt is deductible in the year in which the debt becomes totally worthless. It is important that you begin efforts to collect the debt now in order to provide evidence to prove the debt's worthlessness. Finally, you don't have to exercise incentive stock options (ISOs) if you're subject to AMT.

CHAPTER 11

RETIREMENT PLANNING:
THE BUILDING OF
THE NEST EGG

Many people don't take retirement planning seriously. In fact, some people spend more time planning their summer vacation than planning for their life's ambitions—which is through proper retirement planning. Don't become one of these people.

Unlike years ago when people did not live as long as they do now, having sufficient funds during retirement wasn't as big an issue as it is today. The old stereotype existed. You work for a company for 40 years, have a retirement party thrown in your honor, receive the gold watch, retire to the front porch, spend time on the rocking chair and wait until your number is called.

Retirement planning is much more complicated today than it ever was. The trick is to retire to something, not from something. In fact, if you equate life expectancy to 90 years, and you retire at age 60, you will need funds to satisfy the last third of your lifetime. The only trouble is you will have to earn enough money during the second third (30 years) to fund both the middle and latter thirds of your lifetime (60 years)!

Where can these funds come from? You have Social Security (which was designed to supplement existing retirement plans from employers), your investable assets and the income it delivers and your pensions and other monies you receive on a regular basis.

This is tricky, considering that most people forget to factor inflation into their calculations. Inflation can erode purchasing power. With a 3.5 percent inflation rate, your expenses will double approximately every 20 years. If you make mistakes during your working years, you can combat them by working longer, or changing your investment strategy. As you approach retirement, those options become limited. And once you reach retirement, they are almost gone.

Approaching retirement can be dangerously scary. That's because it is rare to feel comfortable and financially prepared regardless of how much you have accumulated during your working years. The key issues you need to address in beginning this process are the following:

- How long will your retirement last?
- How much will your living expenses increase over time?
- How much income are you likely to need from your personal investments?
- How much can you leave behind to your heirs?

The Process

There are two sides to retirement planning, the buildup of the wealth (contributions) and the disbursement of the wealth (distributions). It is never too early to begin building the nest egg. The sooner you start, the less you will need to contribute on an ongoing basis.

The buildup of the wealth can be accomplished through many different plan types. To make it easy, let's break them down into three types: qualified plans, non-qualified plans and retirement plans.

<u>Contributions</u>

Qualified Plans

Qualified plans (QP) are generally employer-based plans. These include defined benefit plans and defined contribution plans.

In a defined benefit plan, the employer promises a retirement benefit or pension, which can be based on age, years of service or both. The employer sets up a master account for all employees and bears the investment risk on this account. Individual employees do not have their own accounts. If the numbers don't work out as planned, the employer must make up the difference. The number of defined benefit plans has dropped dramatically over the last 25 years for this reason.

Typically, a defined benefit plan pays a retirement benefit based on a formula that multiplies a percentage factor, say 1.5 percent, by the total number of years you worked for the company. The resulting percentage is multiplied by the average salary you earned during your final or highest paid years with the company. Under this formula, an employee who worked 35 years with a company and had a final average salary of $60,000 would be entitled to a pension benefit of $31,500 a year or 53 percent of the final salary. Benefits could also be paid out in a flat amount or adjusted according to the maximum annual benefit.

Since the defined benefit plan is based on age and years of service, the older you are, and the longer you have worked at an organization, the larger your annual contributions can be. That is because you have a shorter time horizon to accumulate funds. With a defined benefit plan, you will know what benefit you will receive, but the contributions are based on what you are entitled to at retirement. That's why the contributions will be larger for an older person with the defined benefit plan.

In a defined contribution plan, the employer pushes the burden of investment risk to the employee. That is why these types of plans are more popular now than defined benefit plans. With a defined contribution plan, a separate account is established in the employee's name. The employee owns this individual account and knows what the account balance is all the time. Since the risk is with the employee, the employee must do a good job of managing that money.

Here, the contribution the employee makes is defined,

but the benefit is not since it is based on the investment income earned over the years. Unlike the defined benefit plan where the employer makes good on the funds if the account is short, the defined contribution plan's benefit is based on how well the employee invests over time. No particular benefit level is promised to the employee when that person retires.

Contributions to the plan can be made by you, your employer or both. Gains or losses to the account will adjust your account. Forfeitures (when employees leave the company before they are vested in the plan) may also be rolled into your account at the discretion of the company. The benefits you ultimately receive will depend on the contributions made to the plan by you and your employer and on the investment returns you achieve on these contributions.

Generally, defined contribution plans are called participant directed plans since they allow you to allocate your investments among a variety of options. Contributions are made with before-tax dollars and earnings are exempt from federal taxes until you begin withdrawing the funds.

Defined contribution plans are generally simpler, more flexible and less expensive for an employer to administer than a defined benefit plan.

401(k) Plans: Your Own Funding Toward Retirement

IRC Section 401(k) is a qualified profit-sharing or stock bonus plan under which you can contribute money, under government guidelines to fund your own retirement. This "cash-deferred arrangement" will allow you to grow tax-deferred money that is earned inside these accounts and allows for this money to be a direct reduction in taxable income in the year you make the contribution.

Employers set up 401(k) plans when the employer wants to shift the investment burden over to the employees and minimally fund the policy. Younger employees stand to reap the biggest benefit since they have many years until retirement and can continue to defer tax on this money until funds are withdrawn.

You are always 100 percent vested in any money you put into the plan.

403(b) Plans

A 403(b) plan, also called a tax-deferred annuity, is a tax-deferred employee retirement plan than can be adopted by certain tax-exempt organizations and certain public school systems. Employees have accounts in a TDA plan to which employers contribute or employees contribute through payroll deduction, similar to a 401(k) contribution.

A nice feature with the 403(b) plan is that in addition to the regular catch-up provision afforded qualified plans and IRAs, a special catch-up provision exists if you have underfunded your 403(b) plan and have been an employee for at least 15 years with the organization. That amount is an additional $3,000 per year for up to five years.

457 Plans

A 457 plan is a non-qualified plan for government employees. They receive the same favorable tax-deferred tax treatment on employee contributions like 401(k) and 403(b) plans.

457 plans also have their own favorable catch-up provision. In this case, the three years prior to the year (and not including) the year of retirement, you can double your contribution for each of those three years (up to annual guidelines). In addition, you can take the "over age 50" catch-up provision as well.

Personal Retirement Plans

Personal retirement plans (PRP) are somewhat different than qualified plans. These plans include individual retirement accounts (IRAs), simplified employee pension (SEP) plans and savings incentive match plans for employees of small employers (SIMPLE).

There are several differences between PRP and QP. PRPs have less stringent government reporting requirements (per ERISA rules) than qualified plans. PRPs do not have to file an annual employer tax return called the Form 5500, whereas QPs do. You cannot borrow from a PRP while you may be able to do so with a QP. PRPs do not qualify for 10-year income averaging while QPs may. PRPs provide for immediate vesting (as soon as contributions are put into an employee's account, they are his or hers), however, with a QP there may be a vesting schedule that forces the employee to wait until the money becomes his or hers. That is set by the employer in advance. Also PRPs may be creditor protected up to a limited amount, while QPs are always creditor protected.

The Traditional IRA

If you have earned income (wages, self-employment and alimony), you can contribute to an individual retirement account (IRA). A traditional IRA is a type of retirement savings arrangement under which IRA contributions, up to certain limits, and investment earnings are tax-deferred until withdrawn from the IRA. You can contribute up to the maximum amount each year, and if you are over the age of 50, there is a special annual catch-up provision that can be added to the maximum contribution.

Anyone can make a traditional IRA contribution, regardless of whether you are covered by a qualified plan. The requirement is that you have earned income to use toward the contribution. The key issue is whether or not it can be deducted on your tax return. Here's the way it works: If you are not covered under a qualified plan from work, you can deduct your IRA contribution regardless of your income. If you are covered under a qualified plan, then income limitations may restrict you from deducting the contributed amount.

A special rule exists whereby if one spouse is covered by a qualified plan and the other spouse is not, then a deductible contribution can be made if the adjusted gross income (AGI) is under that year's threshold.

The Roth IRA

To encourage people to put money aside for the future, the government offers tax benefits to retirement savers. Usually, it's done with pre-tax dollars. However, in 1997, the government provided an alternative—a way to save on an after-tax basis and still grow tax-free. That alternative is called the Roth IRA.

The Roth IRA is the opposite of the traditional deductible IRA. With a traditional IRA, you may deduct contributions within limits and only if you satisfy certain requirements, but all withdrawal limits are fully taxable. With a Roth IRA, you receive no up-front deduction for annual contributions. But, if you meet the tax law's rules, you may withdraw money from a Roth IRA tax-free. You'll owe no tax on the account's investment earnings.

To qualify, a distribution may be taken:

- After you have had a Roth IRA for five tax years.

- On or after the date you reach age 59 ½, due to your death or disability, or for qualified first-time homebuyer expenses up to $10,000. The expenses can be for you, your spouse, your child, grandchild or ancestor of you or your spouse.

And other Roth IRA distributions are taxable to the extent of your account earnings. Unless an exception applies, any distributions prior to age 59 ½ will be subject to the 10 percent early distribution penalty tax in addition to the taxable amount. Unlike traditional IRAs where distributions must begin by age 70 ½, distributions do not have to begin until the holder's death. Lastly, you may roll over on existing IRA into a Roth IRA as long as your AGI for the year does not exceed $100,000. To determine whether converting to a Roth is right for you, ask your financial advisor.

Just like with traditional IRAs, eligible individuals may contribute to the stated maximum each year. However, these amounts represent the maximum amount that can be contributed to all IRAs collectively.

Eligible Roth IRAs contributors can make full contributions as long as your AGI does not exceed the maximum threshold for that year as well.

You need to designate a beneficiary when you open an IRA. This could be your spouse, estate, another person or a group of people. Don't take this lightly, since your choice of beneficiary can affect the beneficiary's tax liability.

Simplified Employee Pension Plans (SEPs)

SEPs are employer-sponsored plans under which plan contributions are made to the participating employee's IRA. These contribution amounts are usually higher than the IRA contribution.

If you are self-employed and earn the maximum amount that you can use toward an IRA contribution, you can put away as much as if you had a defined contribution plan. Therefore, the limits are much higher than what you can put away under a SIMPLE or IRA plan. Also, if you have a slow earnings year, you may be able to skip future contributions whereas in most qualified plans you cannot do that. All qualified plans (except profit-sharing plans) require annual contributions. That could be an exhaustive drain on cash. However, the flip side is that if you continue to miss making contributions, then you will be lacking in retirement monies come retirement age.

Savings Incentive Match Plans for Employees (SIMPLE plans)

SIMPLE IRAs are employer-sponsored plans under which plans contributions are made to the participating employee's IRA. Tax-deferred contribution levels are higher than for IRAs but probably lower than for SEPs. SIMPLE plans also provide an employer with the flexibility to decide whether to make contributions annually. Lastly, SIMPLE plans provide catch-up provisions (like qualified plans) for those over the age of 50.

Non-Qualified Plans

Non-qualified plans are mainly deferred compensation plans, whereby you agree to defer part of your existing compensation to a later date. This reduces your taxable income for the year. The money is not taxed to you until you begin receiving distributions (like other retirement plans). However, the money remains with the employer until you begin receiving distributions. Also, you are a creditor to the company, and if the company should default, you have to line up with all the other creditors against the company to claim your money. So don't do this if your employer is not in good financial health.

You need to declare in advance of earning your salary or other compensation how much you want to defer and when you plan on taking the money. You can make changes every year to alter your earlier decisions.

Most non-qualified deferred compensation plans are designed to provide key employees with additional retirement benefits over and above qualified plan limitations. This serves as an enticement to hire, and retain key employees to help with the business.

CHAPTER 12

RETIREMENT PLANNING: THE SPENDING OF THE NEST EGG

Now that you worked so hard to save for this major life event, here comes the hard part. Withdrawing money to minimize taxes, take what you need and still have enough to grow at a significant rate to ensure that you don't outlive your money.

Having a properly balanced portfolio will go a long way in determining that you don't outlive your money. You also need to be smart during the process. Pulling out whatever lump sum you need is not the way to ensure that your money will be there many years from now. If you do that, you'll have no way of knowing whether your savings and investments are sufficient to see you through retirement. Since you don't know how long you will live, you will not know for sure how the impact inflation and your rates of return will affect your retirement behavior.

Use reasonable assumptions in making these determinations to support the lifestyle that is within your reach during retirement. Many people want to go overboard during retirement, figuring they never were able to do the things they really wanted to do during their working years. But you need to begin making adjustments during your working years and more so during your retirement years (since there is little room for error at this stage). The goal is to reduce your risk of being too far off the mark when beginning your withdrawal program.

Distributions

The general rule is that distributions from retirement accounts are taxable as ordinary income. Ordinary income tax is the tax you pay on money that you earned from work. Exceptions to this rule are Roth types of accounts, like IRAs, 401(k)s and 403(b)s and also pre-1974 distributions which get taxed at a special capital gains rate of 20 percent (which was the rate in effect at that time).

Money can be withdrawn in a lump sum or as an annuity (payments received over time). Each one has tax implications on amounts you receive. Which one makes the most sense for you? Let's have a look.

IRA Rollovers

You can defer taxes on your lump sum through a direct rollover to a traditional IRA. If you directly roll over your proceeds into an IRA, the money can continue to grow, free of taxes, until you're ready to start withdrawing it. By rolling money into an IRA, you can also control how the assets are invested and how much you withdraw. If you don't have an immediate need for a big portion of the lump sum proceeds, the rollover is usually your best option. Loans from a rollover IRA are not permitted.

Be smart about the rollover. If you don't want any money withheld for taxes, then make sure that your pension rollover is done directly from your pension plan to the IRA. Otherwise, by law, your employer is required to withhold 20 percent of the sum for taxes. Even if you put the money into an IRA, you'll have to file a tax return to get that money back.

Also, you can now do a direct rollover conversion to a Roth IRA from qualified plans, Section 403(b) plans and eligible 457 plans.

You can start as early as age 59 ½ to begin receiving distributions from an IRA without penalty, but you can wait till as late as April 1st of the year after you turn 70 ½.

If you are not sure how to proceed with the rollover when you leave your employer, then keep it there until you seek the advice of a financial advisor. The institution where you want to invest the money should be able to help you accomplish the rollover.

Evaluating Early Retirement Offers

In these perilous times, companies are downsizing like never before. You could be faced with an early retirement decision. Many of these decisions occur at around age 55. These offers usually provide cash severance payments, adjustments to defined benefit plans, or other incentives.

First things first. Determine whether the offer is really voluntary or if firing is inevitable. There are no laws stating that you must take an early retirement offer. However, the company can later fire you, claim that your job description has been eliminated, demote you or make life miserable for you.

It makes sense to decide what you plan on doing going forward. Did you have a burning desire to open your own business, travel, volunteer with your favorite charity, take another job, work in a different field or something else? This opportunity can give you the ability to receive a partial payment against something you really want to do.

You will need to do a calculation to determine whether the lump sum will equal the payments you can still receive if you continued working. But lastly, don't make this important decision solely based on financial decisions. All of the above items need to be factored into the equation.

Hardship Withdrawals

Not all qualified plans allow for hardship withdrawals. We said that personal retirement plans never do, simply because you are vested in the money immediately. Therefore, any withdrawal is taxable income immediately.

In order for money to be pulled out as a hardship withdrawal (assuming your employer allows for such withdrawals), the distribution must be necessary in light of immediate and heavy financial needs of the employee and the funds must not be reasonably available from other resources of the employee.

The list of hardship withdrawals meeting immediate and heavy requirements include:

- Medical expenses incurred by you or your spouse or dependents.

- To purchase a principal residence.

- To pay for tuition, educational fees and room and board for the next 12 months of post secondary education for you, your spouse, children or dependents.

- To make payments to avoid eviction or foreclosure on a mortgage from your principal residence.

- Funeral expenses for certain family members.

- To pay for expenses to repair casualty damages to the employee's principal residence.

Loans

Not all qualified plans allow for loans. The plan has to specifically allow employees to access their money via a loan. The benefit of taking a loan is that it allows employees to access their money without incurring any immediate tax liability. Also, loans do not incur the 10 percent penalty that is charged to employees by the IRS for withdrawing or surrendering funds from a retirement account.

Loans must be paid back over five years on a quarterly basis (primary residence loans have a longer time period). If loans are not paid back, they become taxable immediately. Furthermore, if an employee leaves one employer for another, then the loans must be paid back right away.

Loans can be made up to 50 percent of the account balance. The maximum amount of any loan is $50,000. The minimum floor for a loan is $10,000 even if that amount represents more than 50 percent of the account balance.

Interest on the loans is considered consumer interest and not deductible on your tax return, unless it is secured against a home mortgage.

Recent law changes now allow plan loans to be made from a qualified plan to a sole proprietor, an over 10 percent partner in an unincorporated business and an S corporation employee who is more than a 5 percent shareholder in the corporation.

Early Withdrawals from Retirement Accounts

You can receive a "tax" on money that is withdrawn too soon. Early distributions from qualified plans, Section 401(k) plans, Section 403(b) annuities, IRAs and SEPs are subject to a 10 percent early withdrawal penalty. This is on top of whatever tax liability is owed. SIMPLE plans have a 25 percent penalty during the first two years of participation.

Exceptions: As with all retirement plan rules, there are many exceptions to this penalty. Let's look at them now.

The 10 percent penalty does not apply to the following exceptions:

- Made on or after the participant reaches age 59 ½.

- Made to the plan's beneficiary because of the participant's death.

- Attributable to the participant's disability.

- Part of a series of equal distributions (called a 72(t) election) is receiving an equal amount of money over the participant's life expectancy.

- Made upon separation of service (that is, if you leave your job early such as through an early retirement offer)—not applicable to IRAs.

- Made to a former spouse, child or other dependent of the participant under a qualified domestic relations order—not applicable to IRAs.

- To the extent of medical expenses deductible for the year over and above the 7.5 percent threshold for deducting medical expenses.

- To pay health insurance costs while unemployed (IRAs only).

- For higher education costs (tuition, fees, books, supplies and equipment) for the taxpayer, spouse, child or grandchild (IRAs only).

- To pay acquisition costs for a first-time home-buyer participant, spouse, child, grandchild up to a lifetime maximum of $10,000 (IRAs only).

With regard to a series 72(t) election, you must continue distributions for the longer of five years or until the employee reaches age 59 ½. Therefore, if you are age 40 when you decide to receive equal payments of your retirement account balance, you must go till age 59 ½. If you are age 57 when you begin receiving distributions, you must continue it to age 62.

Delaying Your Retirement Distribution

We spoke about the consequences of taking early distributions before the allowable due date of age 59 ½. The flip side is that if you don't take distributions by the required due date (the calendar year in which the employee attains age 70 ½, or the year the employee retires), then the annual distribution that is less than the minimum amount required bears a penalty of 50 percent of the amount not distributed that should have been. You can always take out more than the minimum distribution. The reason being is the more you take out, the quicker the government gets its money from the tax you pay on receiving the distribution.

Minimum Distribution Rules

To determine the required minimum distribution, divide your account balance (as of December 31st of the previous year) by your life expectancy, which is stated on IRS life expectancy tables.

The exception to this rule is that if your spouse is

more than 10 years younger than you, you can use a more favorable life expectancy table that provides for smaller required distributions. Here you can use the actual joint life expectancy of both you and your spouse. The goal is to try to retain your money in your account to continue to grow on a tax-deferred basis.

At the retirement plan participant's death, the minimum distribution to the participant's designated beneficiary is generally based on the beneficiary's remaining life expectancy. If there are multiple beneficiaries in the same account, then the oldest beneficiary's age is used. That's why you want to separate the accounts after the participant's death into individual accounts per beneficiary. This way each person can use his or her own age.

Retirement planning is one of the most important things you can do since you will be earning the money necessary for retirement during one phase of your life and trying to make that money last for the rest of it.

CHAPTER 13

RETIREMENT NEEDS ANALYSIS

Calculating retirement shortfall is a tricky ordeal. For starters, you don't know exactly what you will be spending during retirement. And second, you don't know what you will accumulate until retirement. So many assumptions have to be made.

Going through a retirement needs calculation is a good exercise because it forces you to think things through that otherwise may never have entered your retirement picture until it was possibly too late.

I have included a few worksheets for you to complete to better prepare you for your retirement shortfall. After all, if your resources exceed your needs, you'd be in great shape. But, typically, that is not the case for many individuals.

Retirement Planning Balance Sheet

This form will help you sort through the assets that you will own and liabilities you will owe at retirement. You need to list these values in today's dollars.

Retirement Expense Worksheet

This form helps you sort through the expenses in today's dollars of what you will likely incur during retirement. It then adjusts for inflation to make it a realistic number during retirement.

Retirement Resources Worksheet

This form helps you determine what income sources (i.e., pension and Social Security) you will have to offset the expenses needed at retirement. You will need to find out what your pension amount will be from your employer and your Social Security amount (which you can find out directly from Social Security). In fact, Social Security will send you annual statements indicating how much you will retire on at your retirement age.

Retirement Shortfall Worksheet

This form states the shortage of funds you will need at retirement. This is an amount you can either save annually or accumulate in a lump sum. In any event, you will need to accumulate these funds if you want to retire in the lifestyle you have determined in advance. If you feel that this cannot be done, then you need to make adjustments to your retirement objectives. You can retire at a later date, retire on less funds per month or year or take a part-time job during retirement.

Analyzing Your Results

If your estimated surplus or shortfall is a small percentage, say 1 or 2 percentage points of your projected budget, your needs and expectations are essentially in balance. However, if your projections show a large shortfall or surplus, you may want to go through the exercise again just to make sure you haven't overlooked some detail or made some math error.

If you find no error and still have a large surplus, you can sleep well knowing that you have the ability to substantially increase your annual spending. To be safe, however, you should redo the worksheet assuming lower investment returns, even if you were conservative the first time.

This further analysis gives you an indication of how sensitive your spending ability is to changes in the returns on financial assets.

Obviously, if your figures produce a significant budget shortfall, you should consider whether to change your assumptions. Perhaps you can curtail your spending to get your retirement plan back in balance. It's possible, of course, that your projected investment returns are overly conservative and those higher return assumptions will close the gap. However, before "fixing" your budget shortfall by assuming higher investment returns, reread the investment sections so you know just exactly what would be involved.

Worksheet #1:
RETIREMENT PLANNING BALANCE SHEET

Part A: ASSETS

1. Cash and Cash Equivalents   *Fair Market Value*

a. Checking accounts   _____

b. Saving accounts   _____

c. Money market accounts   _____

d. Life insurance cash values   _____

TOTAL Cash/Cash Values   _____

2. Retirement Plans   *Current Balance*

a. IRA   _____

b. Keogh   _____

c. Section 401(k)   _____

d. Section 403(b)   _____

e. Other defined contribution   _____

TOTAL Retirement Plans   _____

3. Investments   *Fair Market Value*

a. Portfolio investments   _____

1) Money market instruments   _____

2) Fixed-income securities   _____

3) Common stocks   _____

4) Mutual funds   _____

5) Passive investments   _____

6) Real estate (passive)   _____

7) Active businesses   _____

TOTAL Investments   _____

4. *Personal Assets*	*Fair Market Value*	*Adjusted Basis*
a. Primary residence	_____	_____
b. Other real estate	_____	_____
c. Household contents	_____	_____
d. Automobiles	_____	_____
e. Other	_____	_____
TOTAL Personal Assets	_____	_____

Part B: LIABILITIES

1. *Short-Term Liabilities (12 mo. or less)*	*Balance Outstanding*
a. Consumer credit (credit card & open charge accounts)	_____
b. Personal notes payable	_____
c. Loans from life insurance policies	_____
d. Notes guaranteed	_____
e. Other	_____
TOTAL Short-Term Liabilities	_____

2. *Long-Term Liabilities*	*Balance Outstanding*
a. Mortgages on personal residences	_____
b. Loans against investment assets	_____
c. Loans against personal residences	_____
TOTAL Long-Term Liabilities	_____

3. *Other Liabilities*	*Balance Outstanding*
a. Deferred taxes	_____
b. Alimony, child support, etc.	_____
c. Judgments, etc.	_____
TOTAL Other Liabilities	_____

Part C: SUMMARY   *Fair Market Value*

1. Assets   _____

Total Cash and Cash Equivalents   _____

Total Retirement Plans   _____

Total Investments   _____

Total Personal Assets   _____

TOTAL ASSETS   _____

2. Liabilities   *Balance Outstanding*

Short Term   _____

Long Term   _____

Other   _____

TOTAL LIABILITIES   _____

NET WORTH (Total Assets – Total Liabilities)

                    (A)*   _____

*Use **(A)** on **Worksheet #2: Part B: Retirement Resources** in Line 6.

Worksheet #2:
RETIREMENT EXPENSE WORKSHEET

Part A: Estimated Retirement Living Expense

<u>Annual</u> *(In Current Dollars)*

1. *Food*   _____

2. *Housing:*

a. Rent/Mortgage payment   _____

b. Insurance (if not included in a.)   _____

c. Property taxes (if not included in a.)   _____

d. Utilities   _____

e. Maintenance (if you own)   _____

f. Management fee (if a condominium)   _____

TOTAL Housing   _____

3. *Clothing & Personal Care*:

a. Yourself   _____

b. Spouse   _____

c. Dependents   _____

TOTAL Clothing & Personal Care   _____

4. *Medical:*

a. Doctor   _____

b. Dentist   _____

c. Medicines   _____

d. Medical insurance (to supplement
Medicare)   _____

TOTAL Medical   _____

173

5. *Transportation:*   *(Annual)*

a. Car payments   _____

b. Gas   _____

c. Insurance   _____

d. License   _____

e. Car maintenance (tires and repairs) _____

f. Other transportation   _____

TOTAL Transportation   _____

6. *DIscretionary Expenses:*

a. Entertainment   _____

b. Travel   _____

c. Hobbies   _____

d. Club fees and dues   _____

e. Other   _____

TOTAL Discretionary   _____

7. *Insurance*   _____

8. *Gifts and Contributions*   _____

9. *One-Time Expenses*   _____

10. *Income Taxes* (if any)   _____

11. *Total Annual Expenses*   _____

12. *Inflation Adjustment Growth Factor: (see table)*

_____ (Line 11) x _____ (factor)

13. *Total Capital Need at Retirement*   *In Future Dollars*

                          = $ _____

INFLATION FACTOR TABLE

Number of Years Until Retirement	Factor
5	1.2
10	1.6
15	1.9
20	2.4
25	3.0
30	3.7
35	4.7
40	5.8

Part B: Retirement Resources

	Current Dollars	Times Inflation Factor	Future (Retirement Age) Dollars
1. Estimated annual living expenses at retirement age			$_____
2. Annual pension income	$_____	_____	= $_____
3. Plus annual Social Security benefits	$_____	x _____	= $_____
4. Subtotal of projected pension and x Social Security income (add lines 2 and 3)			$_____
5. Shortfall (if expenses are greater than income) that must be funded out of personal savings/investments (subtract line 4 from line 1)			$_____

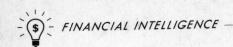

6. Multiply (A) by 17   17 x $_____

7. Equals amount of savings/investments in
future dollars that need to be accumulated by
retirement age to fund retirement $_____

(A) This factor takes into account the retirement net worth
determined from Worksheet #1.

Worksheet #3:
RETIREMENT NEEDS SHORTFALL CALCULATION

1. Line 13 from Part A $_____

2. Line 7 from Part B $_____

3. Difference: (Line 1 – Line 2) $_____

CHAPTER 14

ESTATE PLANNING

Estate planning is the process of organizing your financial and personal interests, in accordance with prevailing laws, so that *your* wishes are met with a minimum of inconvenience and expense to your family. Estate planning also can assure that your estate incurs the minimum possible estate tax.

Effective estate planning need not be complicated. It has several straightforward objectives, including:

- Minimizing the problems and expenses of probate; avoiding potential family conflicts, where possible; passing on your estate in accordance with *your* wishes.

- Providing your spouse with as much responsibility and flexibility in estate management as desired, consistent with potential tax savings.

- Providing for the conservation of your estate and its effective management following the death of either or both spouses.

- Minimizing taxes at the time of death as well as estate taxes after death.

- Avoiding leaving the children too much too soon.

- Providing for adequate liquidity to cover taxes and other expenses at death without the necessity of a forced sale of assets.

- Providing for estate management in the event of the incapacity of either spouse.

- Organizing all-important papers affecting your estate plan in a location known to all family members and to review them at least annually.

Most estate planning objectives can be accomplished by hiring an attorney. You will just be responsible to provide that attorney with your thoughts and concerns.

Where There's a Will, There's a Way

A will is a document that specifies how to divide property, names a guardian and executor for your estate, passes through probate court and alerts creditors of your death.

It can be changed by amending it with codicils, can be handwritten (holographic) or recited from an oral transcript (non-cupative).

You don't need a will to pass property. Property can be passed by titling it a certain way, such as joint tenancy with right of survivorship and placing it in various instruments (trust).

Guidelines for what should be included in a will are found at the end of this chapter.

Letter of Instructions

A letter of instructions is not a legal document like a will. In some ways, it can be more important than a will. Here, you have a lot more flexibility in both the language and content. Your letter is a good place to make your true desires known, specify what you want to happen after your death and include those items not addressed in the will. Essentially, you will state your personal wishes and final comments, but your heirs will be very grateful if you include details about important financial matters.

The letter of instructions plans out exactly what should be done. For example, you would start out with a section on the "first things to do." This could include contacting acquaintances and organizations, including Social Security, the bank and your employer. Arrangements with funeral home will need to be made, providing your lawyer's name and telephone number, calling the newspapers to receive obituary information, locating your life insurance policies, location of cemetery and funeral parlor, present details of your wishes and any arrangements you have made and provide the funeral director with specific facts about you.

Your investment information should be included as well. For your stocks, provide the companies, name(s) on certificates, number of shares, certificate numbers, purchase price and date and location of certificates. For your bonds, gather the names of the issuer, issued to, face amount, bond number, purchase price and date, maturity date and location of certificates. For your mutual funds, give the companies, name(s) on account, number of shares or units and location of statements and certificates. For your other investments, list amounts invested, to whom issued, maturity date, issuer and other applicable data and location of certificates and other vital papers.

For your primary residence, list information about the home. Include in that the name(s) listed on the deed: in whose name, address, legal description, other descriptions needed, lawyer at closing and locations of statement of closing, policy of title insurance, deed and land survey. Concerning the mortgage, include the date taken out, amount owed now, method of payment and location of payment book or statements. If there is life insurance on the mortgage, list policy number, location of policy and annual amount. For property taxes, include amount and location of receipts. Regarding the house, include initial buying price, purchase closing fee, other buying costs (real estate agent, legal, taxes) and home improvements. List improvements, what each consisted of, cost, date and location of bills and for renters, provide lease location and expiration date.

For funeral instructions, specify whether *or not* you would like to have any of the following done: donate organs, public viewing (or wake) and burial. State whether your remains should be buried or cremated. Also specify what type of service should be performed and where the graveside should be located. Specify where memorial gifts should be given or whether to omit flowers, and if prearrangements have been made with a mortuary, give details.

A copy of a letter of instructions is in the back of this chapter.

Understanding Trusts: It's as Easy as A-B-C

The ABC trust arrangement is designed to enhance family wealth by minimizing estate taxes after the death of both spouses. The ABCs stand for the following: a Type A trust is the marital trust or power of appointment trust. Type B is the bypass trust, also called the exemption equivalent or credit shelter trust. Type C is the qualified terminal interest property trust or QTIP.

The marital trust allows for the passing of an unlimited amount of property to the spouse. A bypass trust is designed to contain property that sidesteps or bypasses the surviving spouse's or beneficiary's estate. Where one spouse has most of the assets, those assets should then be transferred to this "poorer" spouse to try to provide sufficient assets so he or she has ample assets to fund the bypass trust. A QTIP trust is a trust that qualifies for the marital deduction as made by the executor on the decedent's estate tax return (Form 706). The key point here is that the QTIP qualifies for the marital deduction even though its property neither passes to nor is controlled by the surviving spouse.

Using the A/B Trust Arrangement

The A/B trust uses one trust, the A trust, as a marital deduction and a second trust, the B trust, as a bypass trust. The A trust contains the assets subject to the marital deduction. The B trust is intended to take advantage of the unified credit against estate taxes. The credit equals exemption equivalent (maximum amount allowed by law) of assets that will be held in the bypass trust. By not using the B trust, you would be wasting an opportunity to successfully rid your estate of up to the maximum allowable amount.

If you want to achieve zero estate tax after the first death and provide the surviving spouse with the powers over all or none of the other assets, you would then help them place the remaining assets into the A trust. The key benefit of this planning is that the surviving spouse can have access and benefit (though restricted compared to an outright ownership of the assets) without those assets being later taxed in the surviving spouse's estate.

Here's how it works. John and Jane Smith have been married for 40 years. Both are U.S. citizens. John and Jane decide to set up an A/B trust. Assume John dies first. After his death, the assets bypass Jane and go to a named beneficiary. Upon Jane's death, she gets to pass the maximum amount of property to any beneficiary estate tax-free. Thus, the family successfully passed the maximum amount of property thus saving a significant amount of estate tax. A side note is that Jane has the right to receive the income and assets of the B trust if those assets are needed for her support. Also, an unlimited amount of property can pass to Jane. Thus, property is not subject to estate tax at the death of the first spouse. However, the assets remaining in the A trust will be included in Jane's estate because Jane has a general power of appointment over these assets at the time of her death.

A general power of appointment allows the spouse, Jane, the right to take the property of the trust for herself, her husband John, others or to give the trust property to her estate. The general power of appointment, as the trust A name indicates, qualifies for the unlimited marital deduction if it can be exercisable by the surviving spouse, Jane, alone and under all circumstances. Practically speaking, this is accomplished by including this power in Jane's will. Therefore, the right to appoint Jane must be unconditional.

Several rules exist for general powers of appointment trusts. They:

- Must provide the surviving spouse with all of the annual income.

- Provide a power that can only be exercisable by the surviving spouse during life or at death, or both where it can be exercisable in favor of the spouse, the spouse's estate or the creditors of the spouse's estate.

Where Do QTIPs Fit?

A QTIP would enter the picture if a marital deduction would be created with an amount in excess of the exemption amount at the death of the first spouse (which is funded within the B trust), but for which a general power of appointment in the surviving spouse would not be warranted. QTIPs are common when dealing with multiple marriages whereby the decedent wants to benefit his or her own children from those earlier marriages, and not benefit the current spouse's children, since property left outright to the surviving spouse can be directed to his or her own children and not to the decedent's children. From a planning technique standpoint, the QTIP is valuable because the decedent can control the assets long after he or she has left this world.

Several rules exist for QTIP trusts. They:

- Must provide the surviving spouse with all of the annual income.

- Cannot give anyone a power to appoint any of the property to anyone else while the surviving spouse is alive.

- Require the executor to make some or all of the property qualify for the marital deduction.

- Must include in the survivor's estate the portion of the assets elected to pass tax-free under the marital deduction.

The benefit received by the executor in deciding whether some or all of the property should qualify for the marital deduction is that with this added flexibility, he or she may determine if there is a tax benefit to be gained by paying tax in the first estate.

Since annual income must be provided to the surviving spouse, it is important to fund the trust with income producing assets. For example, non-income generating real estate, small business owner stock, which pays little or no dividends, would not be appropriate property to be placed into the trust. The reason is that the surviving spouse must be given an interest that is supposed to produce income consistent with its value.

What you should look for is for the surviving spouse to be given the power within the will or trust to convert non-income producing property into income producing property. The flip side of QTIPs involving small business owner stock exists when a family member, other than a surviving spouse, is active in the business. The QTIP provides for that other family member.

Establishing the ABC Trust Through a Will

The A/B/C trust can be established through a will, which is also called a testamentary trust. However, a drawback does exist pertinent to any drafting of a will. And that is, the testamentary trust will be subject to probate. If life insurance were payable to this trust, there could be a delay in getting the funds there.

Differences Between a General Power of Appointment Trust (Type A) and a QTIP (Type C) Trust

A significant difference exists between the general power of appointment and the QTIP trust. The general power of appointment possesses a required marital deduction and can be exercised by the surviving spouse by provisions found in the will. The surviving spouse dictates the ultimate disposition of property. This differs from the QTIP, whereby the executor of the QTIP trust can make an election (it is not a requirement) for the marital deduction. Here, the decedent dictates the ultimate disposition of property, which can be many years after he or she died.

As a result, the QTIP trust is generally favored by attorneys and estate planners alike, over the general power of appointment trust because:

- The decedent retains control over the disposition of the QTIP trust assets upon the death of the surviving spouse.

- The QTIP provides more flexibility in that the executor can make a partial election or a full election to utilize a marital deduction for a QTIP trust, even if the entire trust could qualify for the election.

- The executor is given a chance to clean up mistakes made by being given a second go-round to make changes between the date of death and the filing date of the return, which is when the election must be made.

The general power of appointment trust may work better than the QTIP if:

- A trust is desired to provide stability of management.

- The surviving spouse desires to make lifetime gifts from the trust.

Tax Issues

Gift tax. Since the grantor is setting up the trust and has the power to terminate the trust, gift tax is not payable.

Estate tax. Since the decedent has the power to appoint him or herself as a beneficiary of the trust, the trust assets are includable in his or her estate. However, since these assets qualify for the marital deduction, they would not be subject to estate tax for the decedent. Assets that would not qualify for the marital deduction would then be included as part of the bypass trust. These assets would be includable in the grantor's estate, but would not be taxed on the estate level, since the tax on these assets would be equal to the unified credit. Finally, since the surviving spouse would not receive any part of the principal, since he or she can only receive interest, these assets would not be included in your estate.

Income tax. Since the grantor can ultimately control the assets transferred to this revocable trust during your lifetime, any income generated by the trust would be income taxable to him or her. At death, income generated from the assets would be taxable to the trust if left to accumulate, or the income beneficiary if income were distributed from the trust.

Trustee's Role

This individual is responsible to manage and invest the assets placed into trust during the lifetime of the grantor, generate income for the beneficiaries, be the recipient of life insurance payable to the trust, or property poured over from the decedent's will. This individual needs to act prudently as a fiduciary, serving the ultimate beneficiaries of the trust. The trustee receives a fee for this service.

Planning Your Inheritance

Those who expect to inherit a significant estate should ask their benefactor to create a trust for their benefit, preferably a spendthrift trust. A trust fund set up for an individual is a private transaction, which can protect the principal from one's creditors (and from those of your descendants), from creditors of your estate and from becoming marital property available for a divorce settlement arrangement. Moreover, your parents, grandparents and ancestors can bequeath up to the maximum IRS amount, which can be sheltered from future transfer taxes in your estate and that of other descendants. If you expect a large inheritance, you can even be trustee of these types of trusts as long as you do not have unlimited discretion to make distributions of trust principal to yourself.

The Generation-Skipping Transfer (GST) Tax

Use of the generation-skipping transfer tax can also substantially reduce the overall wealth transfer tax. Know that the GST is an additional tax over and above the estate tax. The GST was traditionally used as a device to save federal gift and estate tax by keeping property out of the taxable estates of the members of the intermediate generation. The beneficiary could be the trustee, have all the income, invade the principal for needs and control the distribution of the property as long as the beneficiary did not have a general power of appointment. Now, the generation-skipping transfer tax considerations of such transfers must also be examined.

There are three levels where GST techniques are useful. First, if you stand to inherit a substantial estate from a parent and already have a substantial estate of your own, a generation-skipping trust would be set up for your parent's property for the benefit of you. Such a trust would allow your beneficiary the use and enjoyment of the inherited property, together with protection against creditors, divorce courts or bankruptcy. The amount subject to the GST exemption will also be excluded from the beneficiary's already substantial estate. Although your parents may pay gift or estate tax, you do not pay estate tax or GST tax on the exempt inherited property at death. Furthermore, no estate tax or GST tax is paid by your children or future issue, depending on the term allowed for the trust.

Secondly, a generation-skipping trust may be used when parents wish to minimize transfer taxes in a child's estate but still give the child the use and benefit of the property, or when the parents wish to protect the property from a spendthrift child, or from being subject to loss through a child's divorce or bankruptcy. In these situations, a generation-skipping trust would be set up to provide income to the child for life, but with the principal being preserved for subsequent distribution to grandchildren.

The trust can continue through the grandchildren's lives (and for great-grandchildren as well), avoiding transfer tax in each generation, subject only to the limitation on the maximum life of a trust under state law. In the case of many estates, however, the generation skip occurs as a result of the death of a member of the intermediate generation before such member receives full ownership of the gift or inheritance, as when a trust is provided for a child until he or she attains age 30, and that child dies before attaining age 30 leaving grandchildren surviving.

Thirdly, you may wish to make direct transfers to a grandchild or other skip person for the beneficiary's education, support or enjoyment, or in order to avoid tax in the estate of the intervening generation. Gifts that immediately benefit grandchildren will generally be subject to the GST tax unless they qualify for donor generation-skipping exemption or the annual exclusion.

Any gift or estate taxes, which become due, are paid and the maximum allowed is transferred in trust to establish a generation-skipping plan. If your spouse consents, double the maximum gift may be transferred in this fashion. The funds are accumulated by the trustee and paid to or for the benefit of all of one's descendants. The effect is to defer for a considerable amount of time (often well over 100 years) the payment of transfer taxes.

These trusts should not permit any descendant who is trustee to have the absolute, unfettered power to distribute principal amounts as this could forfeit tax benefits and creditor protection. It is better to name someone who is not a beneficiary as trustee or co-trustee. He, she or they should have authority to make payments to beneficiaries.

Beneficiary Designation

Planning for your beneficiaries is an extremely important and often-overlooked detail you must adhere to. That's because the potential is too great for things to go wrong and the resulting consequences can be financially devastating. For example, many employers, life insurance companies, brokerage firms and other institutions send requests to update beneficiary forms that often go unanswered or are virtually ignored. By not updating these critical records, retirement plan account holders run the risk of these companies who are looking to make payment, not being able to, because the beneficiaries are no where to be found.

The most common problem is that a retirement plan participant will name a beneficiary under the plan (which was done a while back) and direct those assets inside his or her will to someone else. Beneficiaries are named as a result of a contract to supersede what's stated in the will. Courts have held that a will cannot override a beneficiary designation. Although this conclusion results simply from applying the terms of the retirement plan, some jurisdictions for convenience include an explicit provision in the probate statute.

Other common issues include:

- That the participant states definite dollar amounts, rather than percentages for beneficiaries to ultimately receive.

- Minor children are named as beneficiaries. What ultimately happens is that the court will need a legal guardian appointed by the court to manage their money.

- Participants make changes on their own and don't inform their CPA, their attorney, their banker, their employer or other interested parties.

- Participants are not specific when naming beneficiaries. As a result, there is too much room for misinterpretation.

- Retirement plan participants leaving retirement plan assets to non-spouse beneficiaries, which substantially raises the amount of tax paid.

Guidelines for Letter of Instructions

- ❑ First things to do
- ❑ Cemetery and funeral
- ❑ Facts for funeral director
- ❑ Information for death certificate and filing for benefits
- ❑ Expected death benefits
- ❑ Special wishes
- ❑ Personal effects
- ❑ Personal papers
- ❑ Safe-deposit box
- ❑ Post office box
- ❑ Income tax returns
- ❑ Loans outstanding
- ❑ Debts owed to the estate
- ❑ Social Security
- ❑ Life insurance
- ❑ Veterans Administration
- ❑ Other insurance
- ❑ Investments
- ❑ Household contents
    - List of contents with name of owners, form of ownership and location of documents, inventory and appraisals
- ❑ Automobiles
    - For each car: Year, make, model, color, identification number, titles in name(s) of and location of title and registration

❏ Important warranties and receipts
  - Location and description
❏ Doctors' names, addresses and telephone numbers
  - Including dentist, and children's pediatrician and dentist
❏ Checking & savings accounts
  - Name of bank, name on account, account number and location of passbook (or receipt) for all accounts
❏ Credit cards
  - For each card: company (including telephone and address), name on card, number and location of card
❏ Funeral preferences
❏ Signature and date

Guidelines for Preparing a Will

10-Item Will Preparation Checklist

The following items should be included in a will:

1. Statement that the document is a will.

2. Statement revoking all previous wills.

3. Your full name and location of principal residence.

4. Specific transfers of property to the named beneficiaries.

5. Instructions for dividing the balance of the property.

6. Identify trusts, including the names of selected trustees and successor trustees.

7. Names of guardians and alternate guardians for minor children or special needs relatives.

8. Designation of what monies are to be used to pay death taxes.

9. Names of the executor and backup executor.

10. Signature and date. The will should be signed in the presence of all of the witnesses.

In Conclusion

Americans learned many valuable financial lessons in 2008, many of which will cause them pain for years to come. My hope is that through reading *Financial Intelligence* you have broadened your knowledge surrounding the world of financial planning. Perhaps you quickly realized that successful financial planning goes way beyond just choosing the right investments. Only your own financial intelligence will allow you to meet your present financial needs *and* future goals.

I encourage you to use this book as your personal financial guide. Refer back to it often and mark it up with your notes and thoughts. You are also invited to visit us on the web at www.jacobgoldbooks.com where you can download all the spreadsheets and tables found in this book.

A common pitfall in money management is that many people find themselves underprepared for their golden years; they planned for their immediate goals (like summer vacations) better than they planned for their retirement. I encourage you to reverse that order and become an active participant in your financial life.

Thank you for taking the time to read my book. I hope it helps you in your financial journey.

GLOSSARY

72(t)

A section in the Internal Revenue Code that provides guidelines for early withdrawals from retirement based accounts.

401(k)

A type of qualified, employer-based plan where employees can set aside a portion of their before-tax earnings for retirement. Account balances grow tax-deferred until retirement, at which time distributions are taxed as ordinary income. Some employers offer their employees a match for a percentage of their contributions.

403(b)

A type of qualified retirement based plan that is established by a nonprofit or a public-education organization. Employees can set aside a portion of their before-tax earnings for retirement. Account balances grow tax-deferred until retirement, at which time distributions are taxed as ordinary income.

457 Plan

A type of qualified deferred compensation plan that is established by a state or a local government. Employees can set aside a portion of their before-tax earnings for retirement. Account balances grow tax-deferred until retirement, at which time distributions are taxed as ordinary income.

Adjusted Gross Income (AGI)

An income tax term commonly used to refer to the taxpayer's gross income less specified expenses, such as traditional IRA and employer-sponsored retirement plan contributions.

Agent

A person licensed by a state (or states) to sell insurance.

Aggressive Growth Funds

Refer to the definition of maximum capital gains funds.

Annual Percentage Rate (APR)

The annual rate that is charged for borrowing, expressed as a single percentage number that represents the actual yearly cost of funds over the term of the loan.

Annual Percentage Yield (APY)

The effective annual rate of return taking into account the effect of compound interest.

Asset Allocation

The process of dividing investments among different asset classes to optimize the risk/reward trade-off.

Asset Allocation Funds

Mutual funds that offer a one-stop fund that include U.S. stocks, international stocks, government bonds, corporate bonds, money market accounts and real estate markets.

Asset Classes

Different categories of investments that include domestic stocks, international stocks, government bonds, corporate bonds and real estate.

Balanced Funds

Mutual funds that maintain a balanced combination of common stocks, bonds and perhaps preferred stocks. Balanced funds offer both income and growth because they hold both bonds and stocks.

Bearish

A term that is used to express a negative investment attitude.

Bear Market

A prolonged decline in stock prices that extends over a period of time. A 20 percent decline in value is a generally accepted indication of a bear market.

Beneficiary

The person who receives benefits or payments from an estate or an insurance policy.

Blue-Chip Stocks

Corporations with some of the highest quality of all common stocks because they are dominant companies that have the ability to pay steady dividends in both good and bad times.

Bond

A debt instrument that is issued by a government, state, city, municipality or corporation. The seller of the bond agrees to repay the original principal amount of the loan at a specified time and agrees to make scheduled interest payments.

Bond Rating

A measurement of quality and safety pertaining to the issuer's financial condition. In other words, an evaluation from a rating agency that indicates the likelihood of the debt issuer's ability to meet scheduled interest and principal repayments. Ratings range from AAA (highest quality) to D (lowest quality).

Bullish

A term that is used to express an optimistic investment attitude.

Bull Market

A prolonged advancement in stock prices that extends over a period of time. A 20 percent increase in value is a generally accepted indication of a bull market.

Cash Flow Planning

The management of the inflows and outflows of a person's day-to-day income.

Cash Value

The equity (savings) component within certain life insurance policies.

Certificate of Deposit (CD)

A short-term deposit through a financial institution that pays a specific interest rate for a specific period of time.

Claim

A demand made by the insured, or the insured's beneficiary, for payment of benefits provided by an insurance policy.

The Consumer Credit Protection (Truth in Lending) Act

A federal law that allows individuals the ability to properly compare credit terms from all lending institutions in order to make meaningful comparisons.

Convertible Bond Funds

These funds are bonds or preferred stock that can be exchanged for a fixed number of shares in the common stock of the issuing company. Convertible bond funds combine features of both stocks and bonds.

Convertible Bonds

A corporate bond that can be converted into stock at a predetermined price.

Corporate Bond Funds

Mutual funds that diversify their holdings in various forms of corporate debt.

Corporate Bonds

A debt instrument that is issued by a corporation and sold to investors. The backing for the bond is usually the payment ability of the company.

Coupon

The interest rate stated on a bond when it's issued. The coupon is typically paid semiannually.

Cyclical Stocks

Companies whose earnings tend to fluctuate sharply with their business's cycles.

Debt Instrument

Also know as a bond. Refer to the definition of a bond.

Deductible

The amount of an insured loss paid by the policyholder. If you have a $500 deductible for auto insurance, you pay the first $500 worth of damages to your car if you are in an accident. As deductibles increase, premiums decrease.

Defensive Stocks

Companies that are considered to be recession resistant. They often sell products that a person eats, drinks or smokes in all types of economies.

Deferred Compensation Plan

A type of employer-sponsored retirement plan where compensation has been earned by the employee but has not yet been paid from the employer. With total direction from the employee, the employer holds the income, invests it and delays the payment for a set period of time that defers the taxation of the income.

Defined Benefit Plan

A type of employer-sponsored retirement plan where lifetime retirement income is provided for the employee through the use of various formula-based models (salary history and duration of employment). The responsibility of contributions, investment risk and portfolio management are of the employer.

Disability Insurance

An insurance policy that provides supplementary income in the event of an illness or accident resulting in a disability that prevents the insured from working.

Diversification

The spreading of risk by placing assets in various types of investments.

Dividend

A distribution of a portion of a company's earnings, decided by the board of directors, to a class of its shareholders.

Dollar Cost Averaging

An investment method that involves regular and routine purchases of a security of equal dollar amounts.

Dow Jones Industrial Average (DJIA)

A price-weighted American index that measures the share price of 30 industrial based corporations.

Durable Power of Attorney

A legal document giving one person the power to act for another person, even if the individual becomes incapacitated.

Earnings Per Share

The total amount of earnings divided by the number of shares outstanding.

Equity-Income Funds

Mutual funds that seek a portfolio of high-dividend paying stocks, convertible securities and bonds.

Estate

The value of items that an individual owns, such as stocks, bonds, real estate, art collections, collectibles, antiques, jewelry, life insurance and anything else of value.

Estate Tax

A federal tax levied on an heir's inherited portion of an estate if the value of the estate exceeds an exclusion limit set by law. The estate tax does not apply to surviving spouses.

Exchange Traded Funds (ETFs)

An index fund that trades like a stock.

Exclusions

Specific situations, conditions or circumstances not covered by an insurance policy.

Fixed-Income Investment

A debt instrument that pays a fixed rate of income per year until maturity.

Generation-Skipping Trust

A type of trust where the assets are passed down to the grantor's grandchildren, not the grantor's children. The assets skip over the children and are passed on to the grandchildren for the opportunity to reduce estate taxes at the grantor's death.

Gift Tax

A federal tax applied to an individual giving anything of value to another person.

Global Stock Funds

Mutual funds that specialize in corporations throughout the world, including the U.S.

Government Bonds

A debt instrument that is backed by the full faith and credit of a government. The government agrees to repay the original principal amount of the loan at a specified time and agrees to make scheduled interest payments.

Government Bond Funds

Mutual funds who own securities that are backed by the full faith and credit of a government.

Grantor

The creator of a trust, meaning the individual whose assets are placed into the trust.

Growth and Income Funds

Mutual funds that seek a balanced stock portfolio of growth as well as current income from dividends.

Growth Stocks

Corporations whose earnings are reinvested in capital projects and therefore normally do not pay a dividend.

Holographic Will

A handwritten will.

Home Equity Loans

A type of loan in which the borrower uses the equity in their home as collateral.

Income Stocks

Corporations where a substantial portion of earnings are paid out in the form of a dividend.

Index Funds

Mutual funds that replicate the stocks of a broad section of the market.

Inflation

The rate at which the prices for goods and services are rising, and subsequently resulting in a loss of purchasing power.

Inheritance Tax

In some states in the U.S., a tax is imposed to those who inherit assets from a deceased person. The rate of tax depends on the value of the property received by the beneficiary and his/her relationship to the decedent.

Insured

The person/organization covered under an insurance policy.

Insurer

An insurance company. Also known as a carrier.

International Bonds

Debt instruments that are issued by corporations and/or governments outside the U.S.

International Bond Funds

Mutual funds that typically invest primarily in high-quality foreign government or corporate bonds.

International Stocks

Stocks of companies that are outside the U.S.

International Stock Funds

Mutual funds that specialize in companies outside the U.S.

IRC Section 179

A section in the Internal Revenue Code that allows for accelerated write-offs of business expenses in a single calendar year.

Irrevocable Trust

A trust with terms that cannot be modified or terminated without the permission of the beneficiary. This type of trust may offer estate tax benefits.

Keogh Plan

A type of retirement plan made available to self-employed individuals or unincorporated businesses for retirement purposes.

Liability

The responsibility for causing injury to someone or damage to property.

Large Cap Stock

A publicly traded company that has a market capitalization of $10 billon or more.

Life Insurance Loan

A loan issued by an insurance company that uses the cash value of a person's life insurance policy as collateral.

Liquidity

The ability to convert an asset to cash quickly without affecting the asset's price. Also known as "marketability."

Living Trust

A trust developed by a person during his or her lifetime. Typically, it is used to maintain control over assets while alive and to control the disposition of them at death. A living trust avoids the probate process and may provide for the immediate distribution of assets.

Living Will

A legal document that sets the guidelines for the medical care an individual desires in the event that he or she becomes incapacitated.

Long-Term Growth Funds

Mutual funds that seek capital gains from companies that have potential for steady growth in earnings. Less volatile, and more consistent than maximum capital gains funds, growth funds aim to achieve a rate of growth that beats inflation.

Marketability

Refer to the definition of liquidity.

Market Capitalization

The market value of a company's outstanding shares. Multiply the stock price by the total number of outstanding shares.

Maximum Capital Gains Funds

Also called aggressive growth funds, these attempt to achieve very high returns by investing in more speculative stocks.

Micro Cap Stock

A publicly traded company that has a market capitalization ranging from $50 million to $300 million.

Mid Cap Stock

A publicly traded company that has a market capitalization ranging from $2 billion to $10 billion.

Money Market Mutual Fund

A mutual fund that invests primarily in short-term financial instruments such as Treasury bills and CDs.

Mortgage-Backed Security

An investment that represents pools of mortgages backed by a specific government agency.

Municipal Bond

A debt security that is issued by a municipality, state or county to finance it capital expenditures. The interest is exempt from federal taxes and from most state and local taxes if you live in the state in which the bond is issued.

Mutual Fund

A diversified, professionally managed portfolio of securities that pools the assets of investors and invest in accordance with a stated set of objectives.

Policyholder

A person/organization that purchases an insurance policy.

Precious Metal Funds

Mutual funds that primarily invest in stocks of gold-mining firms and other companies engaged in the business of precious metals.

Premium

The amount of money paid or payable for coverage under an insurance policy.

Price/Earnings Ratio (P/E Ratio)

A company's current share price divided by the per-share earnings.

Probate

The legal process in which a will is reviewed to determine whether it is valid and authentic.

Publication 17

An IRS publication that provides information on all income and deductible aspects of your personal tax return.

Qualified Retirement Plan

A type of employer-based retirement plan that provides a tax benefit when employees contribute.

Rate

The cost of a unit of insurance; the basis for the premium.

Real Rate of Return

The return on an investment expressed as a percentage after subtracting the effects of taxes and inflation.

Refinancing

The restructuring of debt that incorporates a change to the number of years until maturity and/or the interest rate of the loan.

Required Minimum Distribution (RMD)

An annual amount that qualified plan participants must distribute from their pre-tax retirement accounts once they turn 70 ½ years of age.

Risk

The possibility of loss. The chance that an investment's actual return will be different than expected.

Risk Tolerance

The degree of uncertainty that an investor can handle in regards to the valuation of their investment.

Roth IRA

An Individual Retirement Account that is funded with after-tax dollars and grows income tax-free. Unlike Traditional IRA accounts, a Roth IRA does not require you to take minimum distribution at a specific age.

Savings Incentive Match Plans for Employees (SIMPLE plan)

An employer-sponsored plan under which plan contributions are made to participating employee's IRA. Tax-deferred contribution levels are higher than for IRAs but probably lower than SEPs.

Secured Loan

A debt backed by collateral to reduce the risk associated with lending.

Simplified Employee Pension Plan (SEP)

An employer-sponsored plans under which plan contributions are made to participating employee's IRA. These contribution amounts are usually higher than the IRA contribution.

Small Cap Stock

A publicly traded company that has a market capitalization ranging from $300 million to $2 billion.

Small Company Growth Funds

Also called emerging growth funds, these are a type of maximum capital gain fund specializing in stocks of promising small companies.

Socially Responsible Funds

Mutual funds that limit their investments to companies that are not involved in or produce products that are social or morally controversial.

Speculative Stocks

A company where it's stock price is subjected to a wider swing in share price compared to a typical stock.

Standard & Poor's 500 Stock Index

An index of 500 American corporations that are considered to be an overall representation of the U.S. stock market.

Stock

An equity ownership position in a corporation that provides the possibility for dividends and growth.

Stop-Loss Order

An order that is placed to sell a security when it reaches a certain price.

Tax-Deferred Savings Plans

A savings plan that is registered with the U.S. government and provides deferral of tax obligations until distribution.

Term Life Insurance

A life insurance policy that provides coverage for a fixed period of time. After that period, the insured can either drop the policy or pay annual premium increases to continue coverage.

Testamentary Trust

A trust that is created as a result of explicit instructions from a deceased's will.

Time Horizon

The length of time over which an investment is made or held before it is liquidated.

Traditional IRA

An Individual Retirement Account that generally is funded with before-tax dollars and grows income tax-deferred. Withdrawals are subjected to ordinary income tax and may also be subject to a 10 percent penalty if withdrawn prior to 59 ½. Unlike Roth IRA accounts, a Traditional IRA requires you to take minimum distributions beginning at the age of 70 ½.

Treasury Bill

A short-term debt security issued by the U.S. government that matures between four and 26 weeks after issue. Treasury bills are purchased at a discount and mature at their face value.

Treasury Bonds

A long-term debt security issued by the U.S. government that has a maturity of more than 10 years. Interest is paid semiannually and is exempt from state and local income taxes.

Treasury Note

A mid-term debt security issued by the U.S. government that matures in one to 10 years. Interest is paid semiannually and is exempt from state and local income taxes.

Trust Document

A fiduciary relationship where one party, known as the grantor, gives another party, the trustee, the right to hold title to property or assets for the benefit of a third party, the beneficiary.

Trustee

An individual who holds or manages assets for the benefit of another.

Underwriter

An insurance company employee who reviews applications for insurance to ensure they are acceptable and appropriately priced. Sometimes this term refers to an insurer.

Unsecured Loan

A loan that is issued and supported only by the borrower's creditworthiness, rather than by some sort of collateral.

U.S. Savings Bonds

A bond that offers a fixed rate of interest over a fixed period of time.

Variable Life Insurance

A form of whole life insurance that allows the owner of the policy to allocate a portion of your premium dollars to a separate account comprised of various investment options.

Volatility

The relative rate at which the price of a security or group of securities moves up and down, often in comparison to the price movement of the S&P 500.

Whole Life Insurance

A life insurance policy that remains in force for the insured's whole life and requires premiums to be paid every year into the policy.

Will

A legal document that takes effect at death and indicates who is to administer an estate and how the estate is to be distributed. Wills may contain testamentary trusts as well as instructions for the care of dependents.